THE LEGAL PROFESSION
1991

THE IVANHOE/BLACKSTONE GUIDE TO

THE LEGAL PROFESSION 1991

Edited by

Jenny Fry
Jonathan Grosvenor

Published in association with
BLACKSTONE PRESS

THE IVANHOE PRESS
OXFORD

© 1991 The Ivanhoe Press Limited
Kings Meadow Ferry Hinksey Road
Oxford OX2 0DP
Tel: 0865-791006 Fax: 0865-790776

Associate publisher
Blackstone Press Limited
9–15 Aldine Street
London W12 8AW
Tel: 081-740 1173 Fax: 081-743-2292

ISBN 1 870757 39 4
ISSN 0955–7172

Illustrated by Kevin Kallaugher, David Austin, Tony Holland and Nick Newman.
Typeset by Electronic Type and Design, Oxford.
Printed and bound by Redwood Press Limited, Wiltshire.

British Library Cataloguing in Publication Data

The Ivanhoe/Blackstone Guide to the Legal Profession. –
1991–
1. Great Britain. Law
I. Series
344.1

Contents

v

Part V: Becoming a barrister

Part VI: The qualified career

Part VII: The directory

Foreword

Whenever the calibre of a profession is assessed, as well as the obvious tests of integrity and competence, a measure must be made of its ability to assimilate and adapt to change for the benefit of the users of its services.

Our legal profession's competence and integrity have never been in question as is shown by its central role in our society at home and the large number of those overseas who have incorporated in the structure of their legal profession many of its features. In addition, the many recent enhancements to our structure and methodology have ensured and will continue to ensure that the legal profession's services are more comprehensive and efficient than ever before.

If the profession is to meet the challenge of the future it is essential that we continue to attract a significant number of young people of integrity, intelligence and enthusiasm to our ranks. Equally, as the range of services we offer expands, so it is necessary continually to keep the public informed of the expertise available. As always, this guide assists in achieving these aims and I would like to encourage readers to use it as a starting point for their examination of the legal profession, whether as users or potential members.

Mackay of Clashfern

The Rt Hon Lord Mackay of Clashfern
The Lord Chancellor

Introduction

Every year for the past three years this introduction has noted various changes to the legal profession. 1991 is no exception. Where last year the issue of rights of audience for solicitors was under discussion, this year the focus has moved on to the probable extent of these rights. Where twelve months ago both branches were carefully examining the likely impact of 1992, with its potential for an influx of overseas professionals, today the mechanisms for their absorption are taking shape. Increasing numbers of British lawyers are finding themselves servicing clients on the continent. Solicitors are opening offices in other European capitals or forming links with existing firms and barristers and their clerks are enroling on language courses.

Last year as well, there was a fundamental difference in the perceptions of the student population. Too many law students opted for the bright lights of 'the City' and too few chose to capitalize on the hard work of their undergraduate years by qualifying in one of the two branches of the legal profession. This year it is very evident that the absence of any free lunches in the Square Mile has been absorbed by everyone and the security of either legal qualification, never mind their longer-term potential, has become almost embarrassingly apparant.

For a profession that is so central to the health of our economy, the regulation of our society and the presence of equity in all our lives, this is excellent news. All of the changes of the past few years have resulted in today's newly qualified solicitor or barrister facing a far wider range of career choices and much more flexibility in their working life. Furthermore, as 1992 approaches there is the immeasurable potential of the existing European Community as well as the likelihood of the admission of several more states over the next few years.

With all this change in an already complex area, it is not surprising that there is a significant demand for information on the legal profession. As always, the purpose of the Ivanhoe Guide is to provide an introduction through a series of articles covering the major topics, each written by senior practitioners or officials. However, it must be stressed that this book should be used as a basis for further research as no single publication can give a full treatment of such a large topic. On this point, the excellent new Law Society shop is a good place to start.

As is the case every year, the publishing process would have been much harder and ultimately less successful without the help and support of the Law Society and Bar Council. At the former, Ruth Lawrence, Jenny Goddard, Andrew Taylor and Stephen Harwood all gave invaluable assistance and excellent advice, while at the latter, Susan Blake and Lee Weintroube were similarly expert and supportive.

After publication, Alistair MacQueen and Jonathan Harris at the Blackstone Press have used their extensive contacts to ensure the Guide receives the widest possible circulation. And finally, we must thank all the authors and other individuals who were so generous with their time and who made our role all but superfluous.

Jenny Fry
Jonathan Grosvenor
Oxford

Part I
An overview of the legal profession

A brief history of the legal profession

GARY SCANLAN

Gary Scanlan qualified as a Solicitor and is currently a Lecturer in Law at an English university. He has published numerous articles and reviews in professional legal journals and is the Consultant Editor of *The Legal Executive*. He is the co-author of *An Introduction to Criminal Law, SWOT Criminal Law* and *A Guide to the Criminal Justice Act 1988*, all published by Blackstone Press.

Whenever society creates a need, the expert who can satisfy that need follows. The law is no exception. With the coming of the Norman conquest a ruthless plundering of the riches of the nation began. The Norman kings were interested in strong central government, as this was a necessity if the wealth of the nation was to be effectively exploited. They came across a land where each county and even village ran its affairs based upon local custom and practice. In the early Middle Ages local courts using local custom settled disputes between neighbours without recourse to recognized principles of law. It became a practice for the Angevin kings to send representatives (frequently clerics) to these courts and gradually they began to adopt and impose the customs of particular courts they had visited, and of which they approved, to all such courts. These officials from the King's Court began to develop these nationally applied rules into a systematic set of legal principles that would become the common law, and in doing so created both the King's Court (the Common Law Courts) and constituted themselves a professional judiciary. All this was completed by the middle of the thirteenth century. These national courts began to dispense a system of justice that was superior to the local courts. They provided both a means of aiding the centralization of government and a source of profit to the Crown. The judges received fees from litigants, and in criminal cases persons convicted by the King's judges of serious offenses, known as felonies, forfeited both their lives and their property to the King. The King's courts also enforced the King's rights as the ultimate feudal landlord.

These first judges were recruited from among the clerks in the Royal Household and the Chancery (the department of the Royal Household responsible for the preparing and issuing of the King's Writs). These King's judges are the ancestors of the modern High Court judges. Eventually, the medieval judges would be recruited from the successful advocates who practised in the King's courts.

There were in the Middle Ages three common law courts, each staffed by its own judges and court officials, the courts of King's Bench, Common Pleas, and the Court of Exchequer. Each of these courts had originally an exclusive jurisdiction, but in seeking to extend their 'business' and their fees the judiciary of each of these courts so extended their original jurisdictions that they became indistinguishable from one another, at least as regards the types of cases they would hear.

In each of the courts there were two distinct sets of legal practitioners. There were those who told or narrated the litigant's story in court and those who in the absence of the litigant represented and advised him. At that time all steps in an action had to take place in one of the King's courts and in the presence of the litigant or his representative.

The 'narrators' would become the modern barristers. In the course of time the narrators formed themselves into two distinct grades. The ablest and foremost of them constituting themselves the order of 'Serjeants at Law', the others formed the societies that we now know as the Inns of Court. These 'Serjeants at Law', the most eminent of advocates appointed by patents from the King, were the body of men from whom the judges of the King's courts were appointed. They had an exclusive right of audience in the most prominent and prestigious of the King's courts, the Court of Common Pleas. As the other common law courts fought for their share of litigants' fees, the Court of Common Pleas and the 'Serjeant at Law' diminished in importance until the passing of the Judicature Acts 1873-1875 reorganized the common law courts on the modern footing. From this date, it was no longer necessary for a barrister to be a 'Serjeant at Law' to be appointed a High Court judge (the latter term coming into use from that time). The ' Serjeant at Law' ceased to be.

The junior branch of the barrister's profession regulated themselves and though originally known as 'apprentices' grew in prestige and importance. It was found from the end of the sixteenth century that the law offices of the Attorney and Solicitor General (originally the King's Lawyers) required assistance in conducting legal affairs on behalf of the Crown and the State. Barristers of suitable political sympathies were appointed 'King's Council' and were obliged to place their services at the disposal of the King and the government. This is the origin of the modern QC.

The practitioners who represented the litigant and who advised him generally were attached to each of the common law courts; they were constituted officers of the court to which they were attached and their profession of attorney at law was regulated by the judges of that court. One rival court system to the common law courts which grew up was the Court of Chancery. This court dealt with cases involving property, wills and probate and the application of the body of legal rules that would become known as the rules of equity. Though this court was staffed by legal clerks who were supposed to advise litigants they were held in disrepute. A class of men came into being who acted on behalf of litigants in the Court of Chancery, and who tried to ensure that their clients' interests were promoted, and since they solicited the interests of their clients they became known as 'solicitors'. Eventually this profession was recognized as being the equal of the profession of attorney in any of the common law courts.

In the eighteenth century the branches of these professions of attorney and solicitor formed an association called the Society of Gentleman Practisers in the Courts of Law and Equity, a voluntary association which attorneys, solicitors and a profession known as proctors (individuals who practised amongst other things in the Ecclesiastical Courts) could join. Attorneys frequently became attorneys in each of the three common law courts and on occasion were also admitted as solicitors and vice versa. In 1831, the Society of Gentleman Practisers and other smaller and similar associations formed themselves into the Law Society. This body, though a voluntary association, now regulates the training and conduct of the professional lawyer who is now known as a solicitor. In 1875, with the passing of the Judicature Acts, the common law courts and the Courts of Chancery were amalgamated into the modern High Court. Though at the time the High Court consisted of five divisions, today there are only three divisions of the High Court: the Queen's Bench, the Family and the Chancery division. The professions of attorney and solicitor were, from 1875, practically assimilated. The Law Society had to choose a name for the profession and the practitioners, who could now practise law and give general legal advice and represent the interests of litigants in all the divisions of the High Court. Inexplicably ignoring the more noble and distinguished name of the practitioners of the old common law courts the Law Society selected the less flattering name of solicitor to describe and name the profession. The modern professions of both barristers and solicitors, the nature of the work they now undertake, their likely futures and a discussion of the differences between these two branches of the legal profession are discussed in the articles that follow.

Solicitors

RUTH LAWRENCE

Ruth Lawrence is a lawyer and publisher who has previously been the Law Society's Press Officer and is currently the Head of Publishing and Information Services, looking after publishing and careers promotion for the Law Society.

The solicitors' profession is changing rapidly. Although solicitors have a long tradition, the profession in the next century will be more than ever at the forefront of both commercial and community life. If you choose a career as a solicitor you could equally well find yourself using your knowledge of the law to negotiate a shipping contract in Japan, or to put together a defence in a UK murder case.

So what is the link between solicitors doing such apparently different kinds of work? The answer is the link between a solicitor and a client – a special relationship of trust which requires a solicitor to put his or her client first and foremost. Indeed, this duty is embodied as Rule One of the Practice Rules which all solicitors are required to observe.

Being a solicitor is not about paperwork and a stuffy, old-fashioned, image. It is about young people (over half the profession is under thirty-six) working *with* people – their clients – to provide skilled legal representation and advice; whether that advice is about buying a house or selling a company, paying the rent or getting a divorce. It is a career choice which combines intellectual challenge, professional integrity and working well with people – a combination which adds up to a unique form of job satisfaction.

What do solicitors do?

There are three main areas of work for solicitors: private practice, local and central government, and commerce and industry. Most trainee solicitors enter private practice – in other words, they join a business partnership of other solicitors where, as in many other firms, they can expect to start as a trainee, become an assistant eventually work towards becoming a partner, and so share in the management and profits of the business. The type of work done by solicitors' firms varies enormously. In general practice you could be dealing with housing or social security problems, with divorce or child care, conveyancing and property work, or consumer and business matters. Your work will be as much constructive as problem solving – helping a new business set itself up, drafting a complicated will or trust, drawing up all forms of contract. Many clients stay loyal to the same firm – providing it offers a good service – and someone who first comes to you to have a will drawn up may later bring in other, different kinds of work.

In addition, many firms are tending to specialize more and more. Obvious specialist areas are shipping and insurance law, planning and construction work, financial services, or social security law and related areas. Firms range in size from vast partnerships – usually in the City of London and other large cities – right the way down to one or two person high-street practices all over the country. Whatever appeals to you – a particular kind of expertise, or a particular kind of firm – you will have that chance to develop your own skills within that area: litigation (court work), or perhaps the concentration required in drafting important documents.

Solicitors and 1992

Most students are interested in knowing whether a career as a solicitor will involve them in Europe and the single market. Many solicitors' firms are forging links in Europe – either opening offices there, or working with their European counterparts. Many firms have offices in Brussels, working on EC law. If you are interested in working in such a firm, speak to your careers adviser or look in publications such as the Law Society's ROSET (Register of Solicitors Employing Trainees) for further information.

Local and central government

Several thousand solicitors are employed in local government, where their role is providing advice on the important range of public services a local authority offers: education, planning, social services, transport, to name just a few. Again, the opportunity is there to specialize: on the one hand, as a local government solicitor, you could be advising elected council members before a key meeting, while on the other you could be appearing in court seeking an order to bring a child into care.

Solicitors are also employed in a variety of fields in central government, as part of the civil service, and in the Crown Prosecution Service where they prosecute offenders on behalf of the police. A smaller number of solicitors also work in law centres, which offer a less formal approach to the public and often open at weekends and in the evenings. These, like citizens advice bureaux, also offer opportunities for voluntary and part-time work by solicitors.

Commerce and industry

An increasing number of companies employ solicitors as 'in-house lawyers'. A solicitor's work in commerce and industry is, by definition, commercially based: you will be using an acquired knowledge of company law and business structure, banking and financial matters, employment law and anything else that may be important to the successful running of the business of which you form an important part.

There are no obvious advantages or disadvantages to opting for a career in government, or commerce and industry, as opposed to private practice. It all depends whether you prefer working as part of a structured organization, or within a business partnership.

What kind of people become solicitors?

How you qualify is discussed later on in this book. But apart from the question of passing the right examinations, and getting through articles, the people who are attracted to the solicitors' profession are those who relish the intellectual challenge, combined with the personal contact the job provides. Of all the professions, solicitors stand out in this respect. So, if you are a good communicator and a good problem solver, but also patient and able to cope under pressure, you should find you enjoy working as a solicitor. Above all though, you should have the highest standards of personal integrity at all times, and a respect for the clients who come to you for help, and for the profession of which you form part.

The Law Society

The Law Society is the body which represents and governs solicitors. It agrees the practice rules which all solicitors must pass, as well as actively lobbying government and others for law reform. The Law Society's Careers Office offers general advice to students interested in a career as a solicitor. You will find the office's stands and speakers at exhibitions and conventions in England and Wales throughout the year. The Law Society's annual Careers Recruitment Fair is a successful and widely attended event which attracts both students and solicitors in large numbers.

The future

The range of services solicitors supply is increasing all the time. In addition to the 'traditional fields' solicitors now offer financial services and sell property. A number of important changes are imminent, which will affect the structure and workings of both branches of the legal profession in England and Wales. The future provision of legal services must be influenced by what is in the best interests of justice and the general public. Whatever happens, there is no doubt that as the solicitors' profession moves into the next century the services it offers will be increasingly in demand.

The modern Bar

DAVID LATHAM QC

David Latham is a QC practising in general common law in London. The Chairman of the Bar's working party on pupillage which reported in 1988, he is currently the Vice-Chairman of the Professional Standards Committee of the Bar Council.

John Mortimer has much to answer for. Just when the Bar was trying to impress the world with its modern, forward thinking, computerized image, along comes Rumpole to spoil the picture. Crumpled, crusty, not at all contemporary, but thoroughly convivial, his image appears to cut across all the messages which the Bar's public relation advisers have been sending out to the public. The Bar which they seek to project is dedicated, professional, and properly equipped with all the modern technology which is necessary to provide a service to clients in the modern world.

Properly understood, Rumpole is the best argument for an independent Bar. He is in fact utterly professional; he is dedicated to achieving the best result for his client; he is wholly professional in his approach, particularly in court, where he ignores the judge, and concentrates entirely on the people who matter, the jury. Modern technology is of no interest to him, since it is of no relevance to the way he needs to do his work, for his clients. And his fierce independence would make it impossible for anyone to feel able to employ him, or join him in any comfortable partnership. There remains room at the Bar for people like him; the world would be a better place for more of them.

His importance is, however, for what he exemplifies, rather than for what he is. He is one example of the many facets of barrister which now make up the modern Bar. There are now over 6,000 barristers. They are all specialists in one form or another. A large proportion are specialists in advocacy pure and simple. But more and more, with the growing demands made by the sophistication of legislation, and the complexity of the business and financial world, the Bar provides what might be described as the double specialty, namely the advocate with specific expertise in a particular area of the law. The common factor is advocacy, and the common determination is to do the best for one's client. As a result, whilst Rumpole is able to provide the best for his client without modern technology by reason of the nature of his work, there are those who have to provide a service for government, the City, commerce and many other organizations, where the work requires the use of modern technology as an essential tool; and where it is essential, the Bar uses it.

The Bar is a consultancy profession. The barristers' clients are themselves professionals. As an independent practitioner you ultimately succeed or fail on your own merits, there will be no cushioning provided by others. It is therefore a very competitive profession, from the moment that the prospective barrister becomes a pupil, right through to the end of his career. For those who wish to succeed, it involves a lot of very hard work, often at antisocial hours. Above all, the raison d'être of the barrister, that is advocacy, whether at the highest levels, or indeed the lowest, requires an ability to thrive on adrenalin. Almost every appearance in court has similarities to an examination. And experienced barristers will tell you that the nerves before you go into court get no easier to bear however senior you become.

It is important to underline these fundamental features of a barrister's life before considering the way in which the modern Bar operates. There are specialist areas at the Bar in which court advocacy plays only a small part in the overall work of the barrister. But for the vast majority of the Bar, even the paperwork is a form of advocacy, in the sense that it is either advice directly concerned with the client's chances of success in proceedings, or the drafting of pleadings and other documents which are, in effect, written advocacy, and can have a significant effect on the ultimate outcome of any proceedings. At the end of the day, however, the barrister is judged on his ability in court.

This does not mean that the Bar is populated by actors manqués: whilst there are many areas of the Bar in which the colourful advocate still has his place, there is no doubt that the advocacy of the modern barrister is aimed at being effective rather than flamboyant. Effective advocacy means different things in different contexts; in criminal work it will involve remembering that the jury consists of ordinary people who are likely to be affected by common sense rather than purple passages. For a very large proportion of the Bar, now concerned with commercial work, it will involve the ability to analyse complex factual legal situations; and across the whole spectrum of the work the Bar does, there will always be the opportunity for the sort of intellectual debate which may be involved in taking a point of law through to the House of Lords. Advocacy does not mean simple oral advocacy. The Bar has always drafted the formal documents which go before the court, which may well be vital parts of the way in which a case is presented. Increasingly, evidence, and argument, are taken in written form by the courts: the barrister must therefore be persuasive on paper as well as on his feet. Of the 6,000 barristers who practice, about two-thirds do so from London, the remainder either from the main provincial centres in England and Wales, or in Europe. Barristers' chambers are an essential part of the way in which a barrister can work. Not only do they provide the accommodation and administration necessary for running a practice, but they are usually structured as a team providing essential support for one another, and a logical progression in career terms through from pupillage to pension, whether or not that includes a judicial appointment on the way.

Recruitment to chambers is nowadays dependent upon ability. The Bar recruits from across the spectrum of universities and polytechnics. At least one-third of those who are called to the Bar each year are women. Six per cent of the Bar come from ethic minorities (a higher percentage than that of the ethnic minorities within the community). Those who describe it as elitist are correct, if by this they mean that the profession is one which is a meritocracy; they are wrong if by this they mean that it is now unrepresentative in terms of class, sex or race.

'That's not what I meant by the Scales of Justice.'

Legal executives

IAN WATSON

Ian Watson joined the Institute of Legal Executives after graduating with an honours degree in law. Currently the Secretary, Education and Training, he is well placed to explain the role of this important legal body.

Legal executives are the modern descendants of solicitors' managing clerks – wily and experienced practitioners who long held a place in solicitors' offices. Starting out, literally, as clerks engrossing documents, years of patience and dedication imbued a detailed knowledge of clients' matters and legal procedures. However, with the passing of the quill pen and the arrival of typewriters, duplicators and the paraphernalia of the 'modern' office, the role of the clerk as a procedural expert developed and brought with it responsibility for matters undertaken on behalf of clients.

The legal executive's role

Now legal executives are important members of the team in most solicitors' practices, providing specialist support on procedural and legal matters. The role varies according to the structure of the office, but usually legal executives will be involved in one of the main practice specialisms such as conveyancing, criminal or civil litigation, matrimonial or probate and trusts work. A legal executive will often be responsible for the work of one or more of these specialist areas. Most legal executives are employed in solicitors' partnerships, but they are also found in industry, commerce, and local and national government where there is a department dedicated to legal tasks.

So how does a legal executive differ from a solicitor? Mainly in two ways: status and qualification. Legal executives are employees. Solicitors' practices are constituted as partnerships and legal executives cannot become partners. They do not hold any rights of practice as such. These are limited to solicitors and barristers (and now licensed conveyancers) by statute. However, within the framework of private practice there are few practical limitations on the work which a legal executive can undertake. Client matters can normally be handled from start to finish; experienced legal executives may manage branch offices and sign cheques on their clients' account. In litigation matters, legal executives can appear before judges in chambers and, on certain uncontested matters, may appear in open court on behalf of their firm. However, there is no general right of audience in open court.

The other major difference between legal executives and solicitors is the mode of training. Nearly all solicitors now start their qualification by taking a degree, usually in law, sometimes in another subject, and follow this by a further one or two years' full-time study with the Law Society, before starting their practical experience in earnest in a solicitor's office. A trainee legal executive will start his, or increasingly her, practical training on day one, straight from school or following a change of career direction. They will gain practical experience and will support this by studying simultaneously for examinations set by the Institute of Legal Executives. The connection with the old managing clerks continues. The qualification of a legal executive is still firmly based in the practical world and experience is a vital component of it. However, to keep pace with modern requirements, it is essential to enhance experience by studying the substantive law and legal practice covered by the legal executive examinations.

The Institute of Legal Executives

It was as long ago as 1892 that managing clerks perceived the value of banding together to contribute to their chosen profession and to promote their interests. 291 managing clerks met at the Girdler's Hall in London to inaugurate the Solicitors' Managing Clerks Association, subsequently incorporated in 1928. The modern Institute was formed from the SMCA in 1963 with the support and cooperation of the Law Society. The aim was to provide a full training scheme and a career structure for solicitors' staff. The term managing clerk was, at that time, increasingly adopted and misused by employees who did not have sufficient experience. The term legal executive was introduced so that employers would be able more readily to identify those with experience and qualifications. The first group of legal executives was drawn from experienced managing clerks. However, the Institute's training scheme has become increasingly popular – insofar as examinations ever can be. The examination scheme was revised in 1982 to make it more appropriate to the needs of employers and to the needs of a much wider range of applicant. Over 3,000 new students enrol with the Institute each year and their qualifications and backgrounds range from youngsters with GCSE qualifications, through mature students with long clerical or secretarial experience in solicitors' offices, to law graduates, non law graduates and mature entrants making a change of career. Over 17,000 subject entries were received for the main, summer examination in 1990.

The training scheme
The training scheme now provides for study at two levels: Part I, roughly GCE A level standard, provides a broad introduction to all the major areas of law and legal practice likely to be encountered in a solicitors' practice or in a legal department. Part II is set at degree and professional standard and requires study of four subjects (three law, one practice) reflecting the area in which the particular student is specializing in his or her employment. To qualify fully as a Fellow, students must be twenty-five, and have at least five years' experience in legal practice, including at least two years after the examinations have been completed. Courses are offered at over a hundred colleges in England and Wales and the Institute has also established its own correspondence course service, ILEX Tutorial Services, which provides courses for all of the Institute's examinations and also for the examinations of the Law Society and London University.

The Institute also now offers an introductory qualification called the Preliminary Certificate in Legal Studies. It is aimed at prospective students who do not have the GCSE examinations needed to start the full examination scheme; and also those who simply want a one-year introductory qualification in law and administration relevant to solicitors' work.

Membership
The Institute now has a membership of 20,500, principally in England and Wales, but with substantial branches in Hong Kong and Bermuda. Examinations are regularly taken in a number of Commonwealth countries where the legal system is still based on common law. The numbers of new students have increased steadily in recent years. Changes in patterns of qualification generally and the increased commitment of employers to education and training suggest that this trend will continue. The Institute publishes a monthly journal for members and provides the usual membership services. Its members are subject to a disciplinary code, in addition to the restrictions imposed by the Solicitors' Practice Rules.

Aims

The Institute is proud to be able to offer a career in the legal profession for those who have not, for whatever reason, been able to follow the standard routes to professional qualification. Its examinations have been recognized by the profession. Those who wish to extend their qualification and qualify as solicitors can gain exemption from the academic stage of the Law Society's training scheme by taking appropriate heads of the Institute's examination, and dispensation from articles is allowed to Fellows of the Institute. For those who wish to broaden their qualification by completing a degree, the University of London will grant exemption, head for head, from the Intermediate stage of the External LLB degree, and many polytechnics will give similar recognition in respect of their law degrees.

For the employer, the Institute's training scheme provides a valuable assurance that staff have acquired a grasp of a broad range of legal and procedural principles and a specialized knowledge of at least one area of legal practice and the law relating to it. The overall aim is to give staff working within the profession achievable career goals whilst enhancing and securing the quality of service provided to solicitor's clients.

Part II
The law degree

Why read law?

GARY SCANLAN

Gary Scanlan qualified as a Solicitor and is currently a Lecturer in Law at an English university. He has published numerous articles and reviews in professional legal journals and is the Consultant Editor of *The Legal Executive*. He is the co-author of *An Introduction to Criminal Law*, *SWOT Criminal Law* and *A Guide to the Criminal Justice Act 1988*, all published by Blackstone Press.

This is the ultimate question for the budding law student, and is frequently put to such individuals when they are being interviewed for a place on a degree or professional law course.

The answers which are usually given exhibit certain attitudes which potential law students have, or at least profess to have, with regard to legal studies. Students sometimes state that they wish to study law because they want to help people. They may see themselves as future social reformers, using their dazzling legal skills to combat and correct society's ills. Others less exalted see the law as a meal ticket or as a status symbol, the thinking teenager's BMW. These professed reasons for reading law may have been fuelled by television, books, association with individuals involved in the law or experiences at school and work.

A student may subsequently find such reasons to be illusions. Society remains remarkably resilient to change, status is not what it was and a quick survey of salaries offered in the legal appointments pages of the 'quality' newspapers and professional journals shows that the path to riches for lawyers is narrow and full of pitfalls.

Despite realities, the seminal social reformers, status seekers and gold diggers may arrive at their law schools undiminished in the belief that their reasons for studying law are valid for their particular circumstances and these beliefs will sustain them through their student days and beyond.

Others may be less certain of their reasons for wanting to study law. They may wish to pursue a career as a barrister, legal executive, or solicitor, or any of the professions or occupations for which a legal background may be a necessity, though they are not sure why they wish to pursue such a chosen career or to study law. The fact that a student may have no more than a 'gut' reaction that he/she feels that law studies are for him/her is as good a reason as any for undertaking such a course. At the cost of sounding pretentious or patronizing, young people embarking upon a chosen career do so frequently on the flimsiest of whims and rarely come to harm. Whether the course of studies chosen is the right one is impossible to determine and it is pointless to worry about what has already been undertaken. If the study of law is a mistake it is not a disaster, courses can be changed and what has been absorbed during a course of study is rarely without some value.

To sum up, the fact that you cannot rationalize and express in concrete terms your intention to study law does not mean that your desire to commence legal studies is ill-founded or that you would be unsuitable as a law student. The latter issue anyway can only be determined by embarking upon your legal studies.

If you decide to embark upon a law course take great care in selecting your law school. Write to the schools you are thinking of entering before you apply, asking whether they have open days and, if they do, make sure you attend one of them. If at all possible, when you visit a school make a special effort to talk to the resident students. It is an unfortunate fact of life that many law teachers do not take too great an interest in their students' studies (despite lip-service to the contrary); the nature of the teachers at your intended law schools can and should be ascertained by careful questioning of the 'customers'.

If you obtain a place at a law school in which you are left to your own devices this may not be a total disaster. Though a law school which has teachers who take an interest in a student's studies is desirable, you will find that the crucial element in your success as a law student is the effort you put into your studies. This is perhaps the principal reason to study law. Law is not only an academic discipline but a practical science. A student should from the very first day of his/her legal studies inculcate a sense of responsibility and maturity. He/she should show a sense of independence both of thought and expression. These qualities are in no way dependent upon any law teacher, who can only encourage their development; such qualities must be acquired by the student by his/her own endeavours.

Being a law student involves motivating yourself towards a carefully organized and structured approach to your legal studies. You must master the techniques of reading the many hundreds of reported decisions (or precedents) quickly and extracting from these cases the principles of law that constitute the common law, as well as coming to grips with the many Acts of Parliament which now regulate much of our law. The techniques involved in digesting these materials, which can only be acquired by trial and error, will provide you with the skills that are necessary to the successful professional, irrespective of the career you may undertake.

These skills and qualities involve the ability to digest large masses of material quickly and to apply only the knowledge gained which is relevant to a given situation. To be prepared to be flexible in the approach to the solving of problems is a key quality in any professional person; its cultivation must begin and can be developed at law school. The study of law, if approached in the right frame of mind, will help you to become a confident individual, capable of analysing complex problems, and able to express opinions on situations based upon rational thought and backed up by recourse to a source of relevant information obtained by diligent but effective and discriminating study.

In reality, most law students wish to use both the skills and qualities they have acquired and their knowledge of the law so that they may in future act as legal practitioners and advisers, and their study of law is devoted to this end. This is a laudable and worthwhile aim. The careers in the law that are open to you are discussed throughout the rest of this book and require little extra comment. The satisfaction that can arise from a legal career, irrespective of the prestige or wealth that can be derived, is enough to encourage many a young person to become a law student. Nevertheless, the study of law can in itself be a rewarding task without reference to a future career; you must not feel that law studies lead inexorably to a solicitor's office or barrister's chambers. First and foremost, a law student must commence his/her legal studies as an end in itself.

Finally, it must be said that you may find the study of law boring and lawyers insufferable: the latter is clearly understandable and almost certainly unavoidable; the former, happily for those who are young, is instantly remedied. To leave a law school and terminate your legal studies because you find that they are not for you should be as responsible and mature a decision as your decision to commence those studies, and, if based upon sound reasons, never to be regretted.

Where to study

BOB LEE

Bob Lee is Director of Education at Wilde Sapte, one of the UKs largest firms of solicitors, based in the City of London, specializing in all aspects of commercial law. Prior to joining Wilde Sapte, Bob lectured in law in both a university and a polytechnic.

Even with a recession now upon us, there has never been a time when a good lawyers's services were not valued. The shortage of well-trained lawyers lingers on as we enter the 1990s. On both sides of the legal profession there is still intense competition for places in certain firms and certain chambers. So how do you choose a degree course in law that will place you ahead of the field?

To some extent, the answer to this question is dictated by your A level examination results. These may rule out a degree in law altogether, or they may confine you to an institution which makes a lower level of offer, and these tend to be polytechnics. However, simply because the institution offers lower grades it does not follow that the quality of educational provision is poorer. Their intake may have low grades, but their output may be high achievers. Bear in mind that A level averages may remain low because student choice is relatively uninformed, so that factors such as geographical location may prove more decisive than course content or teaching method in making choices. But let us assume for a moment that all of your examinations are graded at the highest possible level, so that you have a free choice of institution – where do you choose?

Oxbridge?

If this is so, you have to begin by looking at Oxford and Cambridge Universities. There are a number of reasons for saying this. At least for your initial posting following graduation, there are some strategic advantages to being an Oxbridge graduate. Almost irrespective of degree level, it is easier to acquire job offers. Indeed, the notion of finals, with all examinations relevant to degree classification at the end of the third year, makes it more difficult to to degree classification at the end of the third year, makes it more difficult to predict what degree the Oxbridge undergraduate will obtain. But this does not prove a barrier to finding work. In addition you will be taught by well-respected, and often famous, academics. Moreover, both are attractive towns in which to be a student. We have said, however, that course content and teaching method might be more important than location.

The teaching method is certainly rather different. You will be taught primarily by tutors from your college. They will take you for intensive tutorial work which will be based on assignments which you have prepared, and in responding to these your tutor may offer what amounts to a cross between personal tuition and medieval torture. Lectures are held on a university rather than college basis, and attendance, which is optional, may vary considerably depending on the quality of the lecturer. Although the notion of tutoring in this way may seem designed to fit your individual needs, the reality may on occasions be different. Tutors may cover a wide range of subjects, and the tuition may lack the excitement of the more inventive, group-based work of new institutions.

University or polytechnic?

So, Oxbridge is an attractive choice but by no means an automatic one, and, if you are not a self-confident individual, you may feel better suited elsewhere. Presumably you look at universities next and, if that fails, polytechics? Although this is a pattern which many candidates follow, it is not obviously correct. Polytechnics are the first choice for some students because they offer more flexibility of access and tuition. As such they appeal to mature students, for example. They may provide more guidance through the law degree, and pay greater pastoral attention to students. The lecturers may place more emphasis on the teaching element within their job, and may have received a better grounding in educational theory. On the other hand, universities are better resourced for the most part. This may affect the quality of your course, via library provision for example, but it may affect, also, the quality of your student life in terms of accommodation, sports facilities and the like.

These are huge generalizations, and institutions vary across what is called the 'binary divide'. Some polytechnic law schools are ahead of some universities in the quality of their legal education – but some are not. So do you apply to university or polytechnic? The answer is simple. Apply to both.

Read the prospectus for each chosen institution carefully, attempt to visit the place, and try and decide where it is that you will be happy. Three years is a long time to spend in a place which you dislike, and even the fact that it has the top four law professors in the country may not cheer you up very much.

There are still some career advantages in attending a university. Many have long histories and offer a known product; many potential employers will have a university rather than a polytechnic degree, and retain a bias towards the former. But as times goes by, and as recruitment gets tougher, those distinctions become fuzzier. In any case, once in a job, future employers tend to be more interested in what you achieved in that job than where you studied for your degree.

Type of degree

One note of caution: do not imagine that all law degrees are the same. The variety of approaches to the academic stage of legal training are enormous. There are three main camps, however, and it is as well to be aware of these. The first is the traditional pattern of law teaching – sometimes labelled 'black letter' law. This name is intended to imply that the course will not look at many sources beyond law. It will concentrate on law as found in the law reports and statutes, attempting to trace the legal rules or doctrines which flow from these sources. It can be contrasted with the more 'contextual' approach. This name hints that it may be necessary to look at law in its economic, social or political contexts, so that review will not focus on a narrow range of legal sources. Finally there exists a more theoretical approach, increasingly based in 'critical' legal theory, and heavily dominated by a rapidly burgeoning literature on the role of law in modern society.

Now, you cannot be expected to understand these different approaches fully in advance of meeting them, but I do recommend that you attempt to trace the nature of the degree courses for which you apply, because you may relish or hate the prospect of an approach to law which has a heavily philosophical bent. Moreover, the picture is not as clear as I have made out. Comparatively few law schools would advertise themselves as committed to one of the above approaches. Indeed there may be no uniform view within the law school as to which should prevail. So read the prospectus carefully and try and ascertain the nature of the discipline you are actually being asked to study in your 'law' degree.

As to which is best in career terms, the answer may be that there is no one winner. 'Black letter' law may appear to be more relevant, but it may bear little actual resemblance to the work which you will do in practice. On the other hand 'black letter' lawyers would argue that other approaches place too little emphasis on core legal concepts. Remember that the law degree is only the first stage of training for a career in law. A year of study for professional examinations plus periods in articles or pupillage will follow. The best advice is to choose a course which appeals to you. You are likely to succeed at something if you are interested in it. Good luck!

Preparation for the course

CHRISTOPHER RYAN

Christopher Ryan is a Senior Lecturer in Law in the Department of Law at City University. He has taught law at a university in New Zealand and also at Liverpool University, Kingston-upon-Thames Polytechnic, Liverpool Polytechnic and Buckingham University. He is author and co-author of several books on criminal law and company law, and he is also chief examiner for the regulation and compliance paper of the Securities Industry examination under the auspices of The Stock Exchange. He has wide experience of advising students.

If you are embarking upon any course in law this does not necessarily mean that you will finish up in practice as a barrister, solicitor or legal executive. It is still true that the majority of students who set out to obtain a law degree or professional qualification in law do intend to make careers as practising lawyers, but a law degree is an appropriate qualification and as acceptable as an arts or science degree for careers in commerce or industry (as executives, managers, public relations and personnel officers), the civil service, police, military, local government administration, court administration or accountancy. Secondly, if you are thinking about or have made a decision to study law you should know that it will require dedication, application and persistent industry on your part. The study of law requires you to read a vast amount of reported cases as well as commentaries on the law. This necessitates development of such skills as rapid comprehension and the ability to assimilate only material that is strictly relevant, to analyse it and argue by analogy from that material. This means that preferably you should come equipped with the powers of concentration of a surgeon, the commitment of a monastic, and the agility of mind and logicality of a chess grand master. You will get by with lesser endowments or attributes of skill but only through hard work.

The best preparation, therefore, for so rigorous a course is making absolutely certain you know what you are setting out to achieve and why. Only if you are certain that law is the course for you will you be well prepared to do

'It's the day of judgement'

battle with it. To be certain, you need to inform yourself about the course, the legal professions and alternative careers. You need to query why you are enrolling for a law course. If you are someone who is simply following in your father's footsteps or who has been 'pushed' by the upwardly mobile aspirations of parents or by careers teachers, who realize you will not quite make the grade for the medical profession, you are not a student 'well prepared' to study law. In order to test your certainty, but also as preparation, you should at the earliest opportunity apply to a local solicitor and/or to the head of a barrister's chambers for permission to spend a week in the office or chambers observing and asking questions. You should also visit court hearings. Our courts are in the main open to the public. You will not always understand what is going on but the familiarity and the 'feel' that you get from being an observer in local magistrates', county, crown and high courts can be very useful in the early stage of a law course. Do not be shy. Good lawyers need initiative and a touch of audacity, therefore you should try and organize a visit to a solicitor's office and to a barrister's chambers yourself by presenting them with your request in writing. Solicitors' firms are well advertised in telephone directories or on windows in the high street, but the local law society or the Law Society (113 Chancery Lane, London WC2A 1PL. Tel: 071-242 1222) would provide you with the names of firms in your area. Barristers are not so easy to find because they do not have direct contact with the public, but a solicitor or, again, the Law Society, would provide you with the names to contact, or an enquiry could be made to The Senate of the Inns of Court (11 Sough Square, Gray's Inn, London WC1). While the thought of visiting courts may seem daunting it need not be in reality because they are staffed by porters, ushers and court clerks all of whom, provided you are polite and presentable, will be very willing to assist you.

Apart from being certain that you really want to study law, and apart from some degree of familiarity with the process of justice conducted in the courts and the role and world of legal practitioners, there is no crucial preparation prior to the start of the degree course. Many students are advised or think they need to study A level law as a precondition. If you think it will help you make up your mind then go ahead but it is *not* necessary: in fact many law lecturers at degree level would prefer that you had not done so on the basis that a little law learning is a dangerous thing, particularly if such courses simply get you into the habit of rote learning and regurgitation. Most degree courses either have induction courses in the first few weeks or else are designed to ease you into the study of law, so that no A level or other preliminary law course is necessary prior to starting at university or polytechnic.

Familiarity with legal terminology is a useful prerequisite and there are certain oft-recommended books of a general nature which serve that purpose as well as illuminating in a simple way what the legal system, the study and the practice of law are all about. It would help if you read the following before the course starts: Glanville Williams: *Learning the Law* (11th ed. 1982), Stevens, and/or AWB Simpson: *Invitation to Law* (1988) Blackwell. Otherwise choose from: R White: *The Administration of Justice* (1985), Basil Blackwell; P Atiyah: *Law and Modern Society* (1963), Oxford University Press; or R Rubinstein: *John Citizen and the Law*, Penguin Books; J P Derriman: *Discovering the Law*, University of London Press; J Malcolm: *Let's Make it Legal*, Education Explorers.

In relation to legal careers, see B Hogan: *A Career in Law* (1981), Sweet & Maxwell, or R Miller and A Alston: *Equal Opportunities: A Career Guide* (1984), Penguin.

In so far as preparing for the mechanics of study are concerned some help may be obtained from: Bradney, Fisher, Masson, Neal and Newell: *How to Study Law* (1986), Sweet & Maxwell; J Dave and P Thomas: *How to Use a Law Library* (2nd ed. 1985), Sweet & Maxwell, and in particular the first two chapters of any of the SWOT series of study aid books published by Blackstone Press, eg Chapters 1 and 2 of Ryan and Scanlan: *SWOT Criminal Law* (2nd ed. 1989), Chapters 1 and 2 of Taylor's *SWOT Law of Contract* (2nd ed. 1988).

Finally, a law student and a lawyer in practice has to be articulate and skilful with words, therefore participation in debating is good preparation, as is being well read both in the classics of English literature and in English history, especially those aspects relating to the development of our constitution.

To sum up, certainty that the course is right for you, general familiarity with the purpose of law, the legal system, and its personnel and terminology are good enough preparation. However, if combined with a developed fortitude to ask questions, a polished eloquence and some pre-tested ability to discipline yourself to a regular, unsupervised work schedule they would provide an even more useful preparation for a degree course in law.

Part III
Becoming a solicitor

Routes into the profession

RICHARD RAMSAY

There are several ways in which one may become a solicitor. Richard Ramsay, a barrister who is a Director of Cadmus Legal Education, a company providing continuing education for the legal profession discusses these below. The present demand for newly qualified solicitors remains high and shows little sign of abating. Perhaps it all goes to show the truth of the old story about the lone lawyer in the small American town who could get no work at all. When a second lawyer arrived they were both very busy!

'Of the making of lawyers there is no end', Francis Bacon might have said and, of those lawyers, the majority will be solicitors. It is, however, more difficult to say exactly what a typical solicitor does and, in reality, it is impossible to give a simple answer. Many work in the public sector, or in industry and commerce, but the majority are in private practice. Some of these are in 'high street' practices, perhaps sole practitioners or in small firms. Others are in larger firms, possibly in the City, where one alone has some two hundred partners.

Whatever their work, solicitors will have four elements in their education: an academic stage, a vocational stage, a professional stage and continuing education. Little needs to be said about the first part as the subject of law degrees is dealt with elsewhere in this publication. It is, however, worth stressing that, whilst solicitors, like most other professions, have moved to effectively all-graduate recruitment this does not mean that all new entrants are law graduates, or that all solicitors, let alone all those recently admitted, are graduates at all.

The academic stage

For law graduates the matter is relatively simple. As soon as they have completed their law degrees they are eligible to pass on to the next stage. This assumes that they have covered the six 'core' subjects (constitutional law, contract, tort, criminal law, land law and trusts) during their studies but this is almost certain to be the case as they are normally compulsory components. Not all law graduates go on to take the Solicitor's Finals examination or any other professional qualification but the benefit of doing so is considerable.

For the non-law graduate the matter is rather less straightforward in that they must study for a further year on an intensive course, the Common Professional Examination, which involves taking all the 'core' subjects. This can be a more difficult route because the content of the course is very demanding: it takes a full year rather than the traditional academic year. Moreover, it is unlikely that the graduate will be publicly financed once he or she has completed a first degree. Discretionary grants are increasingly difficult to obtain but private support may be available. The course may be undertaken at the College of Law or at one of a number of polytechnics. Intending candidates should realize that, whereas the law degree opens doors to both the Bar and the solicitors' profession, the academic stage is, despite its name, not truly common to both in that different establishments prepare students for the different branches.

Mature students must spend two years on the Common Professional Examination course and have to take eight subjects. They might therefore find a part-time course leading to a law degree an attractive alternative. The law is not a career where age is necessarily a barrier. Well over half of the practising solicitors in this country are under forty and partnerships can be achieved by people in their mid-thirties – sometimes earlier – but maturity can be as important a quality as dynamic youthfulness. There is no doubt, however, that the profession is getting younger, as any perusal of the faces of new partners in a weekly journal such as *The Lawyer* will show.

It is also fair to add here that as many women as men are now being admitted as solicitors and many are encouraged to return to their career after having babies – several City firms now organize creches and perhaps the Law Society should consider the possibility of articles being served in the cradle! A year ago it seemed that there was apparently an ever-open demand for new solicitors and this showed no prospect in the foreseeable future of drying up. Can one afford to be so sanguine now? There are signs of redundancies in conveyancing departments and several firms are cutting back on the recruitment of trainee solicitors. There is less corporate merger and acquisition work but insolvency is on the increase. The need is still greatest in the company and commercial areas. With one of the largest firms trying to recruit over one hundred trainee solicitors a year the new graduate is likely to be much sought after. There is, however, competition for places in the best firms and it should be remembered that offers are made for entry into the firm some two years later.

The vocational stage

To have to think about one's career during the academic stage of one's education may seem a little sudden, but forward planning is necessary. Places for the vocational stage can be swallowed up rapidly and at one time there seemed to be something approaching a trade in places at the College of Law. In 1990 a further college at York opened, in addition to those at Guildford, Chester and London. Students may be as well to go to a polytechnic for their Solicitors' Finals – especially if it is near their home – as the basis of the course is a set of materials supplied by the Law Society which are then fleshed out by one's lecturers.

The Finals course is intensive and there are heavy demands on the student's time and concentration during the year. There is a great deal of material and much of it must be committed to memory. Changes are now in the offing, however, as skills training becomes more important than straightforward black letter law. Attempts are made to ensure that the examinations are relevant to practice but students may find that they cover subjects which they neither wish nor will be required to use in practice. The Finals course is intended to provide a transitional phase between academic life and the world of work. It is helpful to have a commonsense approach to learning at this point.

The professional stage

Where articles are served may determine the whole direction of one's later practice. It is usually possible to spend some time with a firm during a period of 'mini-articles' during a long vacation and this provides a good opportunity for the firm to make a better assessment of students' abilities should they wish to apply later. This is a very effective way for firms to recruit the best people by observing them over a period of time early on. If they are very impressed they may go as far as offering some financial incentives, such as payment towards fees and maintenance during the Solicitors' Finals year. It is possible for students to assess the firm as well, to see if it is the kind of environment in which they feel comfortable. Many firms trawl in universities and polytechnics to attract the best students but if a particular establishment is not on the 'milk round' there is nothing to stop individuals from contacting the firms directly which interest them. Student issues of *The Lawyer* are very useful as a source of information about specific firms and most now publish an elegant brochure for recruitment purposes.

It is up to the individual to arrange articles, but the Law Society has a Register of Solicitors Employing Trainees (ROSET), of which there should be copies in universities and polytechnics. It is always worth seeking the help of the appointments board at educational establishments for general advice.

It cannot be stressed too much that, in the present circumstances of high graduate demand, students should look around carefully before making a decision. Although the period of articles means that trainee solicitors will be required to experience a number of aspects of the solicitors' work, what the firm does depends very much on what the firm is.

Continuing education

Although a barrister is called to the Bar after passing the relevant examinations and eating the relevant number of dinners, solicitors are only admitted to the Roll after they have satisfactorily completed their period of articles. Even this is not entirely the end, for solicitors must now attend a number of courses in their first three years of post-qualification experience. This requirement now extends to the rest of their practising lives (the Bar has, for reasons better known to itself, been very reluctant to extend the concept of continuing education to its members). A few people think of this as a chore but for the vast majority it is a valuable means of developing their knowledge and keeping up to date with the fast moving world of the law today.

The larger firms tend to have a training or education director specifically in charge of trainee solicitors and continuing education. Sometimes they double this with responsibility for recruitment. Other firms delegate these tasks to a partner. The quality of post-qualification education and training may well be a major element in the decision to join one firm or another these days. The continuing education requirement may be satisfied by going on courses provided by public or private trainers (all of them must be approved) but a larger firm is likely to undertake at least some of its training commitment 'in-house'.

The necessary qualities

The Law Society publishes a useful document, *Solicitors. A Career in the Law,* obtainable from its premises at 113 Chancery Lane, London WC2A 1PL. Tel: 071-242 1222. This lists the desirable academic qualities as a good memory, numeracy, a good command of language and the ability to get to grips with a problem. Personal attributes include integrity, the ability to communicate effectively, patience, and coolness under pressure. All those interested in becoming solicitors should obtain this publication, which is enlivened by a number of personal career profiles.

In summary, then, the majority of solicitors will now be law graduates, with some non-law graduates who have decided to 'convert' after their first degree. Some will be mature entrants – for the person over twenty-five already working in a law firm, perhaps in a secretarial capacity, this can be a very realistic route and several training directors are alert to the need to 'talent spot' among the ancillary staff of their firms. Very few school-leavers now try to become qualified directly and this aspect is not dwelt on here. There were, apparently, only eight in 1988. 'A' levels must be obtained at certain grades and after a one year course (the Solicitors' First Examinations) a period of five years in articles is served, of which the first will be spent taking the Solicitors' Finals course.

Finally, there are transfers from members of the Bar, who are required to pass certain examinations, but barristers who contemplate a change may work in a solicitors' office for a period before re-qualifying. Re-qualification for experienced barristers is now to be made much easier. Such a step is obviously desirable for those who wish to reach the pinnacle of the solicitor in private practice – to become an equity partner.

In the present climate of many open opportunities it is almost superfluous to wish the eager candidate, 'Good Luck!' although the path is not entirely without difficulties.

The formal training and examinations

COLIN BEATTY

Colin Beatty is the Senior Policy Executive for Legal Education and Training and Secretary to the Entry and Training Committee of the Law Society. Before joining the Law Society, Colin was director of studies of ILEX Tutorial Services, a distance learning college specializing in home study courses in law and legal practice for the whole legal profession.

The formal training which must be undertaken and the examinations which must be passed in order to qualify as a solicitor are set in two stages: the academic stage and the vocational stage of training. Normally these two stages are completed before entering articles of clerkship for a period of two years.

The academic stage is normally met in one of two ways: by graduating with a qualifying law degree or by passing or being granted exemption from a Common Professional Examination (CPE). The vocational stage is normally met by attending a one-year full-time course of study and passing the Law Society's Final Examination.

The academic stage of training

A person wishing to complete the academic stage of training by graduating with a qualifying law degree must ensure that in the studies at university or polytechnic he or she has attended the lectures and passed examination papers in the six 'core' subjects which are: constitutional and administrative law; law of contract; law of torts; criminal law; land law; and equity and the law of trusts. Failure to pass all of these six papers will result in the student spending an additional year studying for any outstanding papers which will be taken in the CPE set in the May or June after graduating. Normally, students required to pass three papers or less in a CPE will be permitted to prepare for them by following distance learning courses.

The Common Professional Examination set by the College of Law and certain accredited polytechnics is recognized by the Law Society as fulfilling the academic stage of training for graduates in disciplines other than law and for mature students of sound academic achievement.

The majority of graduates in disciplines other than law follow a one-year full-time course of lectures and tutorials commencing in September and ending with examinations set in late May or early June. This one-year full-time course covers the six core subjects.

The examination is set internally and administered separately by each branch of the College of Law and by each polytechnic. The examination comprises one three-hour paper in each of the six core subjects and candidates will normally pass the examination only if they have passed each of the six papers on the same occasion, although there is a referral procedure. Except in exceptional circumstances, no candidate is permitted to attempt the examination more than three times.

In special circumstances graduates in disciplines other than law are permitted to attempt the examination as external candidates, having prepared for the examination by following distance learning courses. When permission to study externally is granted it is always subject to a condition that the student extends the course over two years, writing three papers at the end of the first and the remaining three papers at the end of the second year.

Mature students, ie persons who do not hold a degree or equivalent, normally follow a two-year course of study at one of four polytechnics. This two-year full-time course covers the six core subjects and two additional law subjects which must be approved by the Law Society. Students following the two-year course write four examination papers at the end of each year and must pass all four papers on each occasion, although there is a referral procedure. Only in exceptional circumstances may a mature student attempt a group of four papers on more than three occasions.

Fellows of the Institute of Legal Executives may complete the academic stage of training by claiming exemption from the six core subjects of the CPE by virtue of having passed corresponding papers in the Institute's Part II examinations.

The vocational stage of training

Students will normally complete the vocational stage of training by attending a recognized course at the College of Law or at an accredited polytechnic before attempting the Law Society's Final Examination.

Before attending the course a student must have obtained from the Law Society a Certificate of Enrolment as a student member of the Law Society and a Certificate of Completion of the academic stage of training.

The course for the Law Society's Final Examination is full time, beginning in September and ending with the examination in July of the following year. The aim of the course is to ensure that all student members of the Law Society have a common knowledge of the areas of legal practice which are of greatest importance within the profession. The course also aims to integrate the substantive law studied during a law degree course, or on the course leading to the CPE into the practice procedures student members will encounter in the office during the two years they must serve in articles of clerkship.

The course is thus divided into five legal practice subjects: conveyancing; business organizations and insolvency; wills, probate and administration; family law; civil litigation and criminal litigation; a law subject – consumer protection and employment law; and solicitors' accounts. Although revenue law and solicitors' professional conduct are not taught as separate subjects there is a considerable taxation and professional conduct content within each of the main subjects, and both of these two subjects will be examined in the relevant papers set in the Final Examination.

The Final Examination

The Final Examination is set and conducted by the Law Society and therefore each recognized teaching establishment runs a course designed to meet the requirements of the examination. Students are given course materials which reflect the syllabus set in each paper.

The Final Examination consists of the following papers: conveyancing (two two-hour papers); business organizations and insolvency (one three-hour paper); wills, probate and administration (one three-hour paper); civil litigation and criminal litigation (one four-hour paper taken in two parts); consumer protection and employment law (one two-and-a-half-hour paper); and accounts (one two-hour paper).

Candidates will pass the Final Examination only if they have passed each paper on the same occasion. Like the CPE, there is a referral procedure by which a student who has passed five of the seven papers may attempt on two further occasions the two papers in which he has been referred before being required to sit the whole examination again. Resit examinations are held in the February of each year.

A candidate who passes all the papers in the Final Examination at the first attempt and attains the required standard will be awarded an honours certificate by the Law Society.

Fellows of the Institute of Legal Executives who have completed the academic stage of training are permitted to enter articles of clerkship and prepare for the Final Examination as external candidates following distance learning courses. A Fellow is permitted to sit the examination in the July following the completion of articles.

Are you going to be successful?

There is no doubt that the courses leading to the Common Professional Examination and the Law Society's Final Examination are tough and demanding. A wise academic once told me, 'if an examination is passed by every candidate then it is not worth taking', and the formal examinations of the Law Society are worth taking. In the summer of 1988 seventy-six per cent of those attempting the CPE passed the full examination and seventy-three per cent of those attempting the Law Society's Final Examination passed the full examination. Both of these figures will be higher if referral candidates are included.

The important factor is to approach the courses and the examinations with a positive attitude that you are going to pass. Remember, the examiners set the examination for candidates to pass, not to fail, and the examiners will mark candidates' papers to pass them and not to fail them. Preparing for the examinations is hard work but, as Confucius is reputed to have said, 'you must climb the mountain in order to enjoy the view'.

The practical training
MARTIN AND DIANA ILLER

Martin Iller is a Principal Lecturer at the College of Law at Lancaster Gate and member of the Law Society's Academic Consultative Committee. He has taught on the Law Society's Final Course since 1980. Before going into teaching he was a partner in a West End firm of solicitors specializing in litigation and matrimonial work. Diana Iller is a Senior Lecturer at Ealing College of Higher Education. She was formerly in practice as a community solicitor at a law centre, having completed the new style Final Course in 1980/81. Her specialist subjects are company, employment and welfare law, and she has also acted as a marker for the Law Society Finals in litigation and employment law. She is currently an Associate Examiner in employment law for the Institute of Personnel Management and is a part-time teacher at the Inns of Court School of Law in interviewing and negotiating skills.

What is the solicitors' Final Course?

Entry into the solicitors' profession is controlled by the Law Society, who prescribe the content of the Final Course and set and administer the Final Examination. If you would like advice on the Law Society requirements please contact: The Professional Standards and Development Directorate, The Law Society, Ipsley Court, Berrington Close, Redditch, Worcs B89 0TD. Tel: 0527-517141.

In order to qualify as a solicitor you must have attended a 'recognized course '. The College of Law provides places for over 3,000 students each year at its five branches (Guildford, Chester, York, Lancaster Gate and Chancery Lane). A further 1,000 plus places are available at nine polytechnics (Birmingham, Bristol, City of London, Leeds, Leicester, Manchester, Newcastle-upon-Tyne, Nottingham and Wolverhampton). The Polytechnic of Wales has applied to the Law Society for recognition with a view to providing a Final Course for 1991/2. If you wish to apply there please contact the Central Applications Board (see below) before making your application.

From 1991/2 all applications for Finals Course places will be processed by the Law Society Finals Course Central Applications Board, AD MAK 44, London

SW1P 4YL. Tel: 081-547 2242. The closing date for applications for the *1991/2* course was the 21st December *1990* and for future years the closing date is likely to remain at least that far ahead. Students will be entitled to select up to *four* institutions in order of preference (for this purpose the College of Law is a single institution, but students may indicate the branch of their preference).

The Final Course has existed in its present form since September 1979. Its purpose is to provide a 'bridge' between the academic stage and the period that you will spend in the office as a trainee solicitor. By the time you have completed the course, you will share a common knowledge of those areas of substantive law which you are most likely to encounter in practice.

What subjects will I be studying?

The course comprises the following heads:
* Head A: Accounts
* Head B: The business client
* Head C: The private client
* Head D: Litigation

Head A: Accounts
This is basically an introduction to simple book-keeping with special emphasis on those aspects that concern solicitors, for example, the need to maintain separate office and client bank accounts.
* The examination: one two-hour paper.

Head B(1): Business organizations and insolvency
This covers the basic principles of company and partnership law along with those of corporate and individual insolvency. There is also considerable emphasis on tax.
* The examination: one three-hour paper.

Head B(2): Consumer protection and individual employment law
The consumer protection part of the course covers the basic principles governing contracts for the sale of goods and the provision of services, together with consumer credit transactions. The employment law part of the course comprises a very basic introduction to the law governing individual contracts of employment and statutory claims for unfair dismissal and redundancy.
* The examination: one combined two-and-a-half-hour paper.

Head C(1): Conveyancing

This is the longest course in terms of content and covers practical aspects of the registered and unregistered conveyancing of both freehold and leasehold premises. The emphasis is on transactions rather than substantive law and accordingly much time is spent on matters such as drafting contracts and conveyances, pre-contract and pre-completion searches, and the financing of purchases by way of mortgage. The course also deals, in outline, with town and country planning and security of tenure.

• The examination: one four-hour paper taken in two parts.

Head C(2): Wills, probate and administration

As well as covering the drafting and contents of wills and the rules relating to intestate succession and family provision, you will be taught how to wind up an estate. Considerable emphasis is also placed upon tax considerations.

• The examination: one three-hour paper.

Head C(3): Family law

This head concentrates mainly on the law and practice of divorce, including the financial implications of marriage breakdown and matters relating to children. It also looks at a number of other important family procedures, in particular how to obtain protection from domestic violence and the wider aspects of the law relating to children. Once again, tax consequences are considered where appropriate, and time is also spent dealing, in outline, with the significance of welfare benefits.

Although the emphasis is on marriage breakdown, attention is also given to unmarried couples.

• The examination: one two-hour paper.

Head D: Litigation

This course is in two parts: civil litigation, which deals with claims in contract and 'running down' actions in both the High Court and the county court, and criminal litigation, which deals with the trial of standard criminal offences in a magistrates' court, and to a lesser extent in the crown court. The course also covers basic principles of evidence, both in a civil and a criminal context.

• The examination: two two-hour papers, one on civil and one on criminal litigation. Both papers will include questions on evidence.

Professional conduct
This is also part of the Final Course and aspects of professional conduct may therefore be examined in *any* of the examination papers.

What is the course like?

For many graduates, the Final Course comes as a severe shock to the system. Many students take some time to adjust, so it is as well to be prepared before you start. The most striking differences between the Final Course and your degree are:

*   There is no subject choice. Unlike on a law degree, there are no optional subjects. Furthermore, you will need to cover *all* the course material in equal depth.
*   There is no choice in any of the examination papers. All topics must be revised and each question attempted. Questions are subdivided with an indication of the marks for each section, so that time can be allocated accordingly.
*   There is far more material to be covered. The sheer volume of the course takes some getting used to. It means, among other things, that this is one set of examinations you *cannot* 'cram' for at the last moment. You have to begin absorbing and learning from day one.
*   The course material is self-contained. Whichever institution you attend, each head will be taught from a common set of material consisting of 'core material' notes (which vary from subject to subject; some are little more than lecture outlines, others are virtually a self-contained set of notes) supplemented by case studies which illustrate, for example, the documentation in an undefended divorce suit. Unlike on your degree studies it should *not* be necessary to 'read around' the subject because you will be examined solely on the matters dealt with in the core material notes. You will *not* be required to read case reports, although an occasional short reference may be necessary to support a particular point.

However, it is vital to recognize that the Final Course is not intended to be like an undergraduate course – it has a wholly different purpose. It is a course of basic instruction in common aspects of legal practice which is largely concerned with accurate preparation of documents and communication with other professionals. It is hardly surprising, therefore, that there is no choice and that there is no opportunity for 'in depth' private research (a skill you ought already to have acquired as an undergraduate and which in future will be used for individual casework).

There is no doubt that you will find it a 'hard grind', but practising law is a 'hard grind' and if you are not prepared for that, you are in the wrong career. The Final Course is not perfect (very few courses are!) but if you approach the course with an open mind, are prepared to learn your craft, and accept that much of what you are covering is practically relevant and will be of help to you in articles, there is no reason why you should not gain a great deal from it.

What do I have to do to pass?

In order to succeed you have to pass in *every* paper (the pass mark is fifty per cent), but if you only fail one or two papers and with marks of at least thirty-five per cent, you do not need to resit the whole diet – you may make *two* further attempts at the paper(s) you have failed. (This is known as 'referral'). If you still cannot pass the subjects in which you are 'referred' you must resit the whole examination. Candidates who are resitting the whole examination must take it in July (unless the Law Society gives you a special dispensation); 'referral' candidates may resit in February.

Contrary to popular myth, between sixty-two and sixty-eight per cent of first-time candidates pass in every paper while a further ten per cent or so are 'referred' in one or two papers (which they will almost invariably 'knock off' without needing to resit the whole examination). Although there are no separate statistics maintained, it also seems likely that those who fail the whole examination first time round ultimately succeed. Thus, if you want to qualify and are prepared to work *you will pass*.

Ten useful tips

(a) Time is very short. Work from day one (not Christmas, not even day ten!).

(b) Work a normal eight-hour office day, ie 9.30 to 5.30, five days a week, every week of the course. (You may only be required to attend classes for two or three hours per day, but you should spend twice that time working on your own).

(c) Work effectively – plan your study period, plan your rest periods. Do not attempt to concentrate for longer than one-and-a-half hours. A better time is forty-five minutes, break for ten minutes, then resume.

(d)   Learn as you go and practise your knowledge, eg drafting an affidavit. (Drafting is an area traditionally done poorly by students who may feel, wrongly, that form filling is for people other than solicitors).

(e)   The examination is a test of memory but the mere regurgitation of even correct legal principles will not achieve high marks, although it cannot be stressed too highly that it is essential to demonstrate your knowledge of the basic legal points to the examiner. The law needs to be at your fingertips so that you can use it to give clear, accurate and concise advice to your client (examiner) in a form he/she will understand.

(f)   The examination answers must be directed specifically to the question set and there are no marks for waffle and no time to lose in stating irrelevancies. Do not fill three answer books: fill half of one (at most) with highly relevant material. The client is paying for your time and requires sensible workable solutions to his/her problem, written in plain English in three paragraphs – not a dissertation!

(g)   Do not write madly and blindly for the duration of the examination. The examination paper could be ten sides of closely typed A4 and you must spend at least twenty to thirty minutes reading every word carefully. This is part of the examination process and will result in a clear, structured answer. Your ability to select quickly and carefully the relevant facts is essential, followed by a common-sense assessment of the whole problem leading to the best course of action possible. You will not need to consider the academic question 'What if …?'. Confine yourself to the facts and respond accordingly.

(h)   Do take class tests seriously. Plan out your working time each week depending on tutorials and tests. Aim for at least sixty per cent in tests – if you do average fifty-five per cent or higher during the year in all your papers you are almost certain to pass the real examinations.

(i)   In Head D, Litigation, evidence will perhaps carry thirty per cent of the marks although it is often done poorly. This is understandable to some extent, because it is a practical subject and is difficult to appreciate out of context. However, it might well be the key to a pass and so struggle with it, talk it over with your friends, visit a court to see the rules in operation and think at all times, 'What am I trying to prove and why?'.

(j)   Keep everything in proportion. Remember, there is life after law school – people do survive, do resume their normal personalities and actually quite enjoy themselves again! It is worth it, and taken sensibly it can be almost pleasurable.

What comes after the Final Course?

Once you have completed the Final Course, as well as undertaking two years' articles, during which you will be required to be given office experience in three different areas of practice: broadly commercial, non contentious and contentious, you will also have to attend during articles a special accounts course. This is non-residential and covers business accounts. It is taught by a combination of oral and postal tuition but there is no examination at the end.

Finally, once you are qualified you will have to undergo a minimum amount of continuous education during your first three years of admission. Every solicitor *has* to attend a 'Category A' course in each year of that three-year period. These courses are provided by the Law Society and cover office organization and management, professional conduct and client communication, but on top of this you will have to 'score' not less than forty-eight points (not less than twelve in each of the three years) by attending approved courses run by other institutions. Here, however, the choice is yours: there are a vast range of courses provided by teaching institutions. Each course will have been approved by the Law Society and allocated a specific number of points. All-day courses typically carry eight points and half-day courses four points.

The Future – 1993 and beyond

In May 1990 the Council of the Law Society approved proposals to radically change the structure and content of the present Finals Course. Although the detail is still in the process of being worked out it is envisaged that the new course will place a far greater emphasis on training in practical skills such as interviewing, drafting, advocacy negotiation and legal research. In many respects it will therefore be similar to the current Bar Finals Course. In future it is hoped to abolish the system of centrally set examinations and replace it with a scheme in which the individual teaching institutions will set their own examinations. In addition, students will be required to attend a four week course during articles in which they will receive further instruction in accounts, office management and advocacy.

Training with a large firm

PETER WILLOUGHBY

Peter Willoughby is the Training Partner at Turner Kenneth Brown, a fast growing City firm with offices also in the M4 Corridor, Brussels and Hong Kong. Prior to joining TKB he was Professor of Law at the University of Hong Kong and here he provides an outline of the quality of training that can be expected with a large City practice.

In recent years there has been a great deal of research conducted into law students, their career aspirations and the criteria they apply in selecting potential employers. Not surprisingly, given the way the 'market' for trainee solicitors has developed in the past five years or so, good calibre students feel that they can choose freely which type of firm they want to join and what qualities they are going to be looking for in choosing the right firm for them. The research indicates that the quality of training and the preparation which it provides for future development is one of the most important factors influencing students' choice of firms for articles.

As a result of this message, which many firms of solicitors have received loud and clear, trainee solicitor training is receiving an increasing amount of attention, and this is particularly so in larger firms which have the resources to respond quickly.

At TKB we knew from our own internal research among trainee solicitors that the quality of training on offer was an important decision factor for them. In particular the nature of the 'on-the-job' training that we have long provided is very popular. Our philosophy on this aspect of training is that all trainee solicitors should sit in the same office as a partner or a senior assistant solicitor during the course of articles – but more of that later.

In its broadest sense training with TKB starts before a trainee solicitor joins the firm in that he or she will be sent copies of various introductory guides, one of which will be a general informal introduction to TKB written by previous trainee solicitors, and another of which will be a basic manual providing useful information on what they should bring on the first day (a pen, a mug and some Brasso 'for polishing up the handle of the big front door') and on use of the office facilities and services. The first week will then consist of a structured induction training programme designed to introduce the new recruit to the organization and administration of the firm. This is backed up by a further one day course on basic office and professional skills after the first two months of articles.

The programme of 'live' practical training on which each trainee solicitor then embarks is centred on a series of four or more 'seats' in the firm's various departments. Seats in the major departments (company/ commercial, litigation, property) normally last for six months and during that time the trainee will have his or her own desk in the office of a partner or senior assistant and will have day-to-day involvement in live work. Seats in some of the specialist departments (eg intellectual property/information technology, employment or construction) will normally last for three months. If they wish, for their final six months, trainees can return to one of the departments in which they have previously sat or perhaps go to Hong Kong or Brussels. Supervising partners and solicitors ensure that trainee solicitors are fully occupied and gain a wide variety of experience. While a substantial measure of routine work is essential, every effort is made to delegate responsibility to trainee solicitors, although the extent to which this is possible will depend on the nature of the work and the progress of the particular trainee. We believe in optimizing the degree of responsibility given to trainees because the result of this approach is mutually beneficial: TKB gains from the individual's greater contribution whilst the individual gains in experience and confidence.

We also ensure that trainee solicitors have as much contact with clients as possible and in some cases this will mean that they are given their own files and matters for which they are responsible, supervised as necessary by a partner.

During the whole term of articles, trainees will complete check lists, relevant to the department in which they are working, of activities undertaken and experience gained. These check lists are completed on a monthly basis for review by the trainees principal. Trainee solicitors also receive regular formal and informal appraisals of their progress during each of their 'seats' and are interviewed regularly by the partner with overall charge of trainee solicitors.

Apart from this 'learning by doing' process, the training programme for trainee solicitors will comprise the following elements:

(a)   Opportunities to attend a variety of lectures and courses on legal topics run by external professional training organizations, the Law Society and local law societies.

(b)   An annual internal programme of 'essential professional skills' training for both trainee solicitors and assistant solicitors, which covers:
- an introduction to legal writing and drafting
- the art of effective reading
- the art of effective meetings
- the art of negotiating
- managing interviews
- managing time, paper and yourself.

This training is provided in conjunction with external professional training organizations.

(c)   A training course on the use of Lexis, the computer legal reference database.

(d)   Participation in the regular interest and departmental seminars and lectures.

(e)   Attendance at special 'one-off' seminars and lectures given by partners and assistants on specialized legal topics.

(f)   A basic course in management and professional skills held near the end of the two year training contract for those who intend to remain with the firm after qualifying.

(g)   Attendance at departmental meetings which are held regularly and provide an opportunity for the discussion of the latest developments in the law and different aspects of the work of trainees.

(h)   Participation in the firm's Trainee Solicitor Policy Committee through two representatives (one for each year).

Like many other large firms we now invest a great deal of time and resources in ensuring that trainee solicitors get a comprehensive all-round training. To do this effectively requires a recognition that training in general commercial and interpersonal skills, both by being involved in 'live' work and by being trained by professionals, is as important as acquiring legal knowledge and expertise.

Training with a firm outside London

ALLAN CARTON

Allan Carton, formerly a partner in a provincial firm of solicitors, is Business Development Manager for LawGroup UK, the exclusive national network of high quality regional solicitors' practices. His duties include implementing and continuing to develop the network's quality control review which is a prerequisite of membership.

For many years, the majority of solicitors entered the profession to follow in their fathers' footsteps. Then there was a myth that in order to benefit from a top quality training one had to be articled to a firm in the City. Now, many graduates are once again applying to firms in the provinces, and there are certainly many advantages. In particular, people are starting to look for jobs where they do not have to waste a couple of hours a day (480 hours or the equivalent of twenty days per year – even allowing for four weeks' holiday!) commuting.

But can you get the same range of experience in a regional firm as a City practice? Generally speaking, yes. Within the legal profession there are a small number of niche practices which offer a highly specialized service to a very closely targeted market, and the majority of these are based in the City. However, the provinces offer a very good selection of firms dealing with commercial work and general practice work including legal aid. From the graduate's point of view it is usually considered better to obtain a very broad-based training; specialization can always follow once you are qualified.

What about salaries; are those offered in the provinces at the same level as those in City firms? While they will not be quite as high, they will certainly compare favourably when you consider the lower costs of living.

So how should you decide which practice to apply to? There are a number of factors to consider. You will undoubtedly want to join a firm which you are sure carries out work to the highest standards, but how can you tell? Many practices have established reputations in their area and these are usually a fairly safe bet. However, you might also wish to look at firms which are constantly monitoring their quality. Members of the LawGroup UK network are a good example. They have to undergo a stringent review of their procedures before being allowed to join; this is then repeated annually to ensure that the high standards of management, client care, staff training, and other procedures are being maintained.

You will also want to find out what sort of training is on offer. This will probably depend to a large extent on the size of the firm and the type of work it does. In most large firms there are training programmes in place, many of the smaller practices will send you on commercially organized courses, and the national groupings of firms generally have their own courses arranged for the benefit of members' staff. LawGroup, for instance, runs a series of courses, all of which are accredited by the Law Society.

Most people know whether they are likely to be more comfortable working in large firms or small ones. While the recent trend in the legal profession has been towards merger, there are still plenty of good smaller firms looking for graduates every year. The structure of the firm will probably dictate how much contact students actually have with partners; one could probably generalize that the smaller the firm the more contact you are likely to have with them on a day-to-day basis. You will also find that in the smaller firms your involvement in casework will be maximized and even fairly early on in your training you will be asked to take responsibility for dealing with clients.

Another factor you might consider is your future with the practice. Are you looking at the firm as a short-term prospect; somewhere that you can train but do not propose to stay? If so, then the 'partnership make-up' may not be terribly important. However, if you are thinking about partnership prospects in the future you would do well to find out whether the practice has any expansion in mind; also whether all the partners are young or if some are due for retirement in five or ten years' time.

Once you have decided on the kind of firm you wish to work in, and have been accepted, what can you expect to be doing? It would be unwise to generalize because, although you will get a broad range of experience in most firms, the way each individual practice arranges its articled clerks' progress from one department to another can vary enormously. The length of time you spend in any one department can also vary, but you might expect it to be between four and six months. If you have a particular interest in one field then you should check as early as possible in your discussions with the partners that you will have a chance to work in that department at some stage.

There is one other important factor you should consider before accepting an offer of articles and, unfortunately, it is not something which you can determine from just reading about a firm. You need to decide whether you will actually be comfortable working in that practice. Although it is difficult to tell from just one or two visits to an office, you can usually get an instinctive feel for the atmosphere. If you are not certain, do not commit yourself just because it is the first offer you get; demographic trends show that good calibre graduates will be much in demand and you may well be able to pick and choose.

From my own experience as a partner in a comparatively small firm, and from the insight I have gained into many firms since joining LawGroup, I have no doubt that the quality of work and training offered in many regional firms is equal to that found in London. I would stress, however, that it is vital you find a high quality firm with which to train, regardless of the location you choose, because what you learn now will be the basis on which you build your entire career.

Training in a City practice

ALEXANDRINA LE CLEZIO

Alexandrina le Clezio is Head of Education at Herbert Smith, one of the leading law firms in the United Kingdom. Based in the City of London, Herbert Smith also has offices in Brussels, Hong Kong, New York and Paris. Herbert Smith undertakes a broad range of legal work for both international and UK-based clients and offers its trainee solicitors a comprehensive training programme in each of its three main areas of practice: company, litigation, and property.

Working in a law firm is a challenging experience where innovation and imagination, practicality and common sense need to be combined with a sound knowledge of substantive law. Meeting the requirements of clients goes well beyond merely putting theory into practice.

For this reason, practices run comprehensive training programmes for trainee solicitors from the moment they enter the firm: enabling them to learn about business and commercial considerations as they develop their knowledge and understanding of law and legal practice.

At Herbert Smith, for example there are two major elements in that training programme: practical 'on-the-job' training, where trainee solicitors deal with client work under the supervision of qualified solicitors, and the formal trainee solicitor legal education programme, which is designed to complement and develop practical training.

Practical training

The purpose of practical training is to offer trainee solicitors the opportunity to experience different types of legal work, to get a broad range of experience and to enable them to take a decision on their eventual area of specialization on qualification.

Practical training within the firm is designed to go well beyond the minimum standards set by the Law Society. These require firms to provide experience of law within two major categories covering a variety of legal fields.

Given the breadth of our work, this is not difficult. However, we do feel that trainees need to gain a solid understanding of a particular area and so structure our practical training programme around four six-month placements. The first three are taken in the firm's three main practice areas: company, litigation and property. For the fourth seat, trainee solicitors often choose to go into a department where they hope to practise on qualification or to one of the overseas offices. As they change from one department to another they are also given the opportunity to request work with a particular section such as tax, banking, shipping, insurance or planning. At the same time general training is taken very seriously and we try to ensure that the experience in any one placement is as broad as possible.

In each of their four placements over the six-month period, trainee solicitors sit with either a partner or a senior solicitor. This enables them to see how more experienced solicitors deal with all aspects of a transaction. They will be given two types of work in each of their four 'seats': matters for which they have primary responsibility and matters where they work as part of a larger team. The emphasis is on giving trainee solicitors as much responsibility as they are capable of handling, as early as possible. To help them do that effectively, comprehensive support is given both in terms of close supervision by senior solicitors and by way of technological and administrative assistance. They will also have access to the legal information database via terminals on their desks. The database has been designed by Herbert Smith lawyers for Herbert Smith lawyers and gives easy access to the firm's expertise. So running their own matters becomes a challenging and satisfying area of their work and working as part of a much larger group on major transactions means that they learn how to work with others, to whom they can refer on all aspects of the deal.

The legal education programme

As well as practical training, trainee solicitors attend courses designed specifically for them throughout their two years of articles. Their own legal education programme is designed to complement and develop practical training and is divided into distinct stages, reflecting their development through the two years of their articles. The programme as a whole concentrates on two main areas: legal and business skills and the law and practice associated with each of the departments in which they will sit.

Emphasis is placed on inviting both suggestions from trainee solicitors on suitable topics for inclusion within their own programme and individual input by them within each session. This approach aims to ensure that the programme is relevant to their needs and that practical sessions encourage an active response.

Induction programmes

This more formal training starts the day they join the firm. They then begin an induction programme designed to give them an understanding of the areas of work covered by the firm, the resources and services available to them, including technology, and office practice and procedure. The initial induction programme also gives them the opportunity to get to know one another.

Skills

The skills that they will need to practise as commercial lawyers are introduced in stages throughout their two years in articles. At an early stage they will have a course on the City and its business to introduce them to commercial practice and City jargon. They will learn drafting skills and legal research skills both in the library and on the firm's databases. Further courses in business skills will be dealt with during articles and at various times after they qualify, including communication skills, time management and negotiating.

Law and practice

As they join a new department for the first time, trainee solicitors will also have a short induction course on the law and practice associated with the transactions dealt with in that department. This enables them to understand the structure and development of large transactions and to be better equipped to solve problems. As responsibility for the management of clients and transactions will come early, we take seriously our responsibility to provide support and training to them to enable them to deal effectively with client matters. Throughout their six months in a seat there will be further courses which will be a mixture of information sessions and practical workshops. As far as possible we prefer to run training sessions in the context of mock transactions, providing client instructions and documentation to simulate the procedures which they will meet in the office. So trainee solicitors learn to take instructions, research, advise, take appropriate decisions and negotiate first in a training session and then on behalf of their clients within the context of departmental matters.

Departmental training programmes

In addition to their own legal programme, trainee solicitors within each department attend the training programme for that department. This offers more specialized information relevant to transactions within that department.

Briefing sessions

Groups within the firm in all departments meet regularly in order to exchange information on current transactions, the application of new law and procedure and views on current problems. Every qualified solicitor in the firm is a member of at least one group within his or her own department, and, in addition, some groups span more than one department. Trainee solicitors join the meeting for the group in which they sit and many take an active part, often providing material for discussion.

The future

Training does not cease on qualification. Newly qualified solicitors participate in the legal education programme for the department in which they have decided to practise and, in addition, the training programmes designed specifically for them. These develop their knowledge and understanding of transactions and the skills which they have acquired in articles. Herbert Smith believes that training at all levels is of vital importance to the firm. Training will remain an integral part of career development.

Articles within the smaller firm: for or against?

LESLEY COX

Lesley Cox is the Litigation Partner with Mawby Barrie & Scott, a five-partner Holborn firm with an Anglo-German client base. Fluent in German and with a multidisciplinary approach, Mrs Cox enjoys meeting the challenge of a quality clientele within a personal atmosphere.

Students who are totally convinced that they are corporate man personified may, in their search for articles, gravitate relentlessly towards the City and the multimerger partnership. In so doing, however, they might miss much that is on offer only in the smaller firm.

What is the smaller firm?

Small firms, of course, will vary in size and direction, but, forgetting for the moment the one-man band, it is possible to find good all-round experience within a partnership of less than ten partners. Many such partners will have brought to the firm significant background experience acquired in larger firms, thus providing the student with a good sense of perspective. Provided that a student is careful to check that such a firm can offer relevant experience in all the major areas – and many do – then the student may be agreeably surprised at the quality of training which can be given.

Qualitatively speaking it is a fact that many firms have a clientele crossing the entire spectrum, from the individual on legal aid to the multinational corporate client. Whilst the latter may, themselves, turn to the City for their heavy public company or new issue work, many enjoy maintaining well-established links with smaller firms. Whatever its size a firm is only as well remembered as the service it can offer on a one-to-one basis, and it is in this area of personal attention that the small firm really comes into its own.

For the trainee solicitor, therefore, there is ample opportunity to enjoy client contact right across the board and to experience the attitudes and skills through which the small firm is often very successfully able to compete with its larger counterparts.

It would be wrong, moreover, to think that the small practitioner will necessarily be kept from the mainstream of expansion. Well nurtured contacts and working partnerships with professionals from other spheres can widen horizons to considerable effect. Increasingly solicitors may work in cooperation with barristers, accountants and patent agents to build a formidable team. It is perfectly possible to run an international venture from a relatively individual base.

The personal advantages

Subject again to the proviso that students must check the expertise available, their training is likely to be more 'in depth' within the smaller firm. From the very beginning the trainee solictor will, in a smaller firm, be a vital member of the team. As such the student's training – *your* training – will be a matter of intimate concern to the partnership as a whole. There is little chance here of feeling isolated; you will still have to undertake the chores but you can rest assured that you will always be close to the centre of the action. You are likely to have greater exposure, therefore, not only to a variety of clients, but also to the methods by which partners work. You can be a true apprentice in a way that simply is not possible within the larger organization.

For your part you may find your own unique personal contribution will be that much more readily appreciated from such relatively close quarters.

Type of work

As to the type of work, if you are looking for specialist work – a criminal practice, for example – then you will make your choice accordingly. In a small general practice, however, you are likely to encounter many of the following aspects of work:

Company and commercial work. Whilst you are unlikely to be participating in public takeovers, you may well gain experience in the acquisition and sale of businesses, setting up joint ventures and, most certainly, the preparation of conditions of sale and purchase, distribution and agency agreements, employment contracts and general commercial agreements. You will certainly, too, learn all the basics of company formation.

In *conveyancing* you are likely to deal with considerable domestic transactions, but you will also encounter commercial conveyancing whether involving offices, factories or warehouses. If you remember that the smaller business in a start up situation is likely to turn to the small firm for its legal advice, you will see that the breadth of such advice requires the close cooperation so prevalent within the smaller firm.

If you feel you might enjoy working 'with people', then you will have ample opportunity to assist with their personal dilemmas, be they to do with the drawing up of wills, realistic tax planning (which you are likely to undertake in conjunction with accountancy practices) or in connection with the whole range of problems attendant upon matrimonial breakdown, including custody issues and financial negotiations. *Litigation* can of course embrace just about any type of human or commercial dispute. Thus, since you are unlikely to spend your articles 'assigned' to one enormous – and therefore to some extent restrictive – action (as you might in a larger firm), you will appreciate a huge variety of work (and life!) to which the litigator may turn his hand. If your threshold of boredom is low, then litigation in this context could well be for you.

'He's our legal eagle.'

The drawbacks in perspective

On the down side, you may miss the camaraderie of your peers; you may well indeed be the only trainee solicitor. In this setting, however, even the most senior partner is likely to be approachable and may welcome an exchange of ideas with student staff. Small firms are very adaptable: they have to be.

Finally, on the question of finance, there is little doubt that the small firm will not be in a position to offer the salaries available within the larger practices. What it does offer, however, can be invaluable for your future development and career. Since you will obtain experience in many varied aspects of legal work you will be well placed to make a decision as to the specialist field in which your future may lie. Whatever you decide to do, once your training is complete you will have gained considerable insight into the area of practice development itself, and ultimately it may be within a practice of your own that you find most fulfilment. If, in the meantime, you enjoy your stay, you may be sure that high initiative and a good performance will be readily appreciated for smaller firms depend, more than most, on their trainee solicitors for future staff, and partnership prospects are realistic. You may be somewhat short on the administrative luxuries of life – although not necessarily so – but all in all, for many students, a training within the smaller firm can be rewarding in much, much more than riches.

Continuing professional education

SOPHIE HAMILTON

Sophie Hamilton is the Partner at Frere Cholmeley with the responsibility for training all the firm's professional staff. Frere Cholmeley is a leading European Law firm with over 150 lawyers working from its offices in London, Paris, Brussels, Milan, Monte Carlo and Berlin.

Of the many reasons given by those seeking articles for their choice of law as a profession, its constantly changing nature and its intellectual challenge must rank as two of the most frequent. The necessary concomitant of these two undoubted benefits is the enthusiasm on the part of the lawyer to continue his or her own legal education well beyond solicitors finals, well beyond articles and indeed well into his or her dotage. It is the encouragement of this enthusiasm for continuing to learn which is the responsibility of the training partner and sets the challenge which most law firms now seek to meet.

Consistent with that philosophy, the Law Society recognized in 1985 the importance of training and professional development, and as a result introduced a compulsory scheme of professional education for all newly qualified solicitors. The term 'newly qualified solicitor' then embraced all solicitors in the first three years from admission. The aim of the scheme is to ensure that solicitors recognize the value of updating and enhancing their knowledge skills, thereby delivering a better service to their clients.

In August 1990, the second stage of the continuing education scheme was introduced by the Post Admission Training Regulations 1990. This has wider implications for the profession and necessitates that all solicitors qualifying from August 1987 onwards undergo compulsory training throughout the remainder of their professional career.

The provisions of the scheme can be summarized thus:

(i) Those qualifying between 2nd August 1985 and 1st August 1987 must accumulate a total of 48 points over three years, with no less than 12 points being gained in any one year.

(ii) Those qualifying from 2nd August 1987 onwards must collect 16 points every year.

Categories of course

The courses a newly qualified solicitor has to attend fall into two categories:

* the accredited points carrying courses; and
* the compulsory 'Category A' courses.

Points carrying courses

Only courses organized and delivered by authorized providers carry points. The Law Society has authorized a wide range of private sector organizers in addition to the College of Law, polytechnics and university law schools. A number of firms and consortia of firms have also been authorized so that attending an in-house course arranged by an authorized firm can also earn points towards the overall total. This is particularly valuable since courses can be tailored to meet the needs of a particular firm and its practice. This option is not lost for small firms, who are in many cases getting together to pool resources for training.

How does it work?

The number of points which can be earned by attending an accredited course is determined by the length of the course. Generally speaking, morning, lunchtime or early evening courses are accredited with 1 or 2 points, half-day courses with 4 points, day-long courses with 8 points and courses lasting more than one day with 10 points.

Course subjects

The scheme is sufficiently flexible for courses explaining the practicalities as well as the technicalities of a solicitor's practice to carry points. Courses on legal skills (such as drafting, negotiation or interviewing techniques) can be accredited in the same way as courses on technical subjects. Since the scheme was established, the range of topics covered by accredited courses has widened and now there are few areas of practice which are not covered by accredited courses somewhere in England and Wales.

'Category A' courses

Under the 1985 Law Society Regulations the 'Category A' courses do not attract continuing education points, but are a vital part of the continuing education process. These courses are organized by the Law Society and take the form of a half-day session once a year.

The first and second post-qualification year 'Category A' courses remain the same under the 1990 Scheme, and they are:

Year 1: Effective office and communication skills
Year 2: Professional conduct and ethics

The Law Society attaches great importance to attendance at these courses in the early years of office experience. A substantial number of these 'designated courses' are held at the Law Society's Hall in Chancery Lane.

Year 3 'Category A' course
The change effected by the 1990 regulations is to the third post-qualifications year 'Category A' course, which will no longer be 'handling professional responsibility' but will be replaced by a course based on the Law Society's management kit entitled 'Best Practice'. These courses will no longer be organized by the Law Society, but will instead be arranged and delivered by some external and in-house providers who have satisfied the Law Society that they have the resources and the ability to deliver the course. This course will attract continuing education points.

The training record
Under the new regulations the Law Society no longer expects the solicitor to submit an annual form of return, but they do expect the solicitor to maintain a training record. This will encourage the solicitor to take further responsibility for training and, more importantly, the recording of courses attended. The Law Society or any representative of the Law Society may demand production of it at any time. If a solicitor fails to comply with his or her obligations under the scheme, the Law Society can refuse to issue, or renew, the individual's practising certificate.

Variation of the Regulations

Under the 1985 Scheme an application to vary the Regulations by granting an exemption was based upon the experience of the applicant. However, as it is intended to extend the scheme to the whole of the profession then this will no longer be appropriate. The Law Society may well agree to a deferral under special circumstances, such as, maternity, long-term illness, unemployment or working abroad. It will approach such applications on a flexible, but discretionary basis.

The future

The scheme is still very much in its infancy, and as yet there are no decisions as to when the compulsory continuing education will be extended to include the more senior solicitors. Nevertheless, it is likely that in the near future it will gradually be extended to cover all practitioners on a staged basis. The real challenge for the in-house and private sector providers of training programmes will be delivering suitable advanced training courses for the more senior fee earners.

Notes on qualifying as a solicitor

General

(a) Law graduates do the one-year Law Society Finals (LSF) course.

(b) Non-law graduates must first pass the Common Professional Examination (CPE).

(c) After passing the LSF you serve two years' articles, usually with a firm of solicitors but perhaps in local government, industry or a law centre.

(d) Finally, you are admitted to the Roll of Solicitors.

The Common Professional Examination

(a) This one-year course teaches non-law graduates enough basic law to enable them to go on to the LSF course.

(b) CPE courses take place at the College of Law and at various polytechnics.

(c) Places on CPE courses are in short supply. Apply in time.

(d) Your careers service has application forms and dates.

(e) Obtain a Certificate of Eligibility, from the Law Society. A certificate will not be issued until you have been awarded your degree and have a provisional offer of a place on a CPE course.

(f) Check to see if your degree exempts you from any papers.

(g) The papers cover crime, tort, trusts, contract, constitutional and administrative law.

(h) Most institutions offering the CPE and the LSFC will offer students who pass the CPE at the institution a place on their LSFC.

The Law Society Finals Course

(a) The course is run at branches of the College of Law and at nine polytechnics (see list following).

(b) The College of Law has seventy-five per cent of the places and a long waiting list, so apply in the first term of your degree course.

(c) The polytechnics are slightly less pressured. Obtain details, forms and dates from your careers adviser and apply in your first year.

(d) Many students apply to a polytechnic and the College of Law to ensure a place.

(e)   Unless taking time off after your degree (unwise – you will forget it all!) you must join the Law Society before starting the LSF course.

(f)   Get the enrolment form from the Law Society early in your third year.

(g)   References are asked for and followed up. Make sure those whose names you give are happy to act as referees.

(h)   Contact the Law Society if no reply is received by August.

(i)   On graduating, obtain a Certificate of Completion of the Academic Stage of Training from the Law Society.

(j)   Apply for a grant from your local authority.

(k)   If you apply for a loan from a bank through the Law Society you will be given a more sympathetic hearing.

(l)   The course is tough.

(m)   It cannot be crammed, so attend the lectures and take and use your own notes.

(n)   The mid-session exams are important.

(o)   Past exam papers are free, so use them.

(p)   Given the papers' practical emphasis it is worth attending the lectures which cover practical topics.

(q)   If ill, do not sit the exams, as you are only allowed three attempts. If you must, then at once obtain and submit a letter from your doctor.

(r)   There are seven papers divided into five legal practice papers: conveyancing; business organizations and insolvency; wills, probate and administration; family law; civil litigation and criminal litigation; one law subject – consumer protection and consumer law; and solicitors' accounts.

(s)   The pass mark for all papers is fifty per cent.

(t)   If you score thirty-five per cent to fifty per cent in up to two papers you may resit them twice. Subsequent failure means resitting all seven papers.

Colleges providing recognized courses for the CPE and LSF course

Birmingham Polytechnic, Franchise Street, Perry Barr, Birmingham B42 2SU. Tel: 021-331 5000

Bristol Polytechnic, Coldharbour Lane, Frenchay, Bristol BS16 1QY. Tel: 0272-656261.

City of London Polytechnic, School of Business Studies, 84 Moorgate, London EC2M 6SQ. Tel: 071-283 1030.

College of Law, Braboeuf Manor, St Catherines, Portsmouth Road, Guildford GU3 1HA. (Branches at Chester, London and York). All enquiries to Guildford 0483-576711.

Leeds Polytechnic, Calverley Street, Leeds LS1 3HF. Tel: 0532-462909.

Leicester Polytechnic, School of Law, PO Box 143, Leicester LE1 9BH. Tel: 0533-551551.

Manchester Polytechnic, Aytoun Street, Manchester M1 3GH. Tel: 061-228 6171.

Newcastle-upon-Tyne Polytechnic, St Mary's Place, Education Precinct, Newcastle-upon Tyne NE1 8SP. Tel: 091-232 6002.

Nottingham Polytechnic, Burton Street, Nottingham NG1 4BU. Tel: 0602-413248.

The Polytechnic of Wales, Pontypridd, Mid Glamorgan CF37 1DL. Tel: 0443-480480.

Wolverhampton Polytechnic, Molineaux Street, Wolverhampton WV1 1SA. Tel: 0902-313002.

Colleges providing recognized courses for CPE only

Birmingham University, Edgbaston, Birmingham B15 2TT. Tel: 021-4143344.

Central Polytechnic, Red Lion Square, London WC1R 4SR. Tel: 071-283 1030.

City University, Northampton Square, London EC1V 0HB. Tel: 071-253 4399.

Huddersfield Polytechnic, Huddersfield, Yorkshire. Tel: 0484-516151.

Lancashire Polytechnic, Preston PR1 2TQ. Tel: 0772-22141.

Staffordshire Polytechnic, College Road, Stoke-on-Trent ST4 2DE. Tel: 0782-744531.

Articles

(a) This is a two-year practical apprenticeship usually served with a firm when you are classified a trainee solicitor.

(b) The Law Society imposes and enforces minimum standards to ensure a broad training.

(c) Inevitably your training will reflect the size, location and specialization of the practice.

(d) Large firms have a formal training structure and you are usually rotated through various departments on a series of six-month secondments.

(e) In small firms there is a more informal approach.

Finding articles

(a)   Demand for trainee solicitors is rising faster than the number of places on the LSF course.

(b)   However, most students make multiple applications and so the more popular firms can afford to conduct a rigorous selection procedure.

(c)   The key is information, presentation and timing.

(d)   Find out which firms you want to approach using ROSET (the Register of Solicitors Employing Trainees, a Law Society publication listing over 3,000 firms and other organizations with brief relevant details), law magazines, the Law Society's Recruitment Service (see page 196), and any personal contacts. The law is a 'people' business and so this last is often the most effective.

(e)   The Law Society Code of Practice says no firm should recruit trainee solicitors more than two years ahead.

(f)   Most big firms therefore expect you to apply two years ahead!

(g)   If reading law, this means large law firms mount a roadshow giving presentations in the spring and expect you to apply in the summer vacation of your second year.

(h)   Medium sized and smaller practices, often unsure of their requirements, frequently recruit nearer the time.

(i)   Identify a short list of target firms.

(j)   Send each a CV (or obtain an application form from your careers service) and a brief covering letter requesting an interview.

The Code of Practice

(a)   No interviewing programme for the recruitment of applicants should be initiated before 1st September in the student's final year of degree studies.

(b)   Where representatives of firms of solicitors visit universities or polytechnics to interview applicants, such visits should not start before the beginning of the October term and dates of proposed visits should be agreed in advance with the appropriate careers service in each case.

(c)   Ideally, an offer of articles to an undergraduate should not be subject to a time limit for acceptance. If, however, such an offer does state a final date by which a decision is required (or by which the offer, if not accepted, will be deemed to be declined), that date should not be before

1st November in the academic year in which the law graduate takes degree finals (or the non-law graduate the CPE course) or the expiry of three weeks after the offer is sent, whichever is the latter.

(d) Students will be expected to acknowledge within a day or two the receipt of any offer and if they are able immediately to give a final acceptance or rejection then they should do so. It will, however, be open for the student when acknowledging receipt to indicate that he or she wishes to have time to consider the offer and to state the date by which it is anticipated that a final decision can be given. If such a date is outside the time limit prescribed in the offer, the firm concerned should give sympathetic consideration to extending the time limit accordingly.

(e) Students will be expected not to accumulate offers. These should be dealt with as promptly as possible and students should restrict the number of outstanding offers held at any one time to no more than two. Once a student has accepted an offer, he should tell all other employers to whom applications have been sent and thereafter he should make no further applications.

Information and statistics

Introduction

The information and statistics set out in this chapter and the one in part IV are extracts from the Annual Statistical Report of the Law Society. The report was compiled by Stephen Harwood of the Law Society's Research and Policy Planning Unit who has produced quite the most comprehensive analysis of the profession available to date. What follows here can only be a subjective selection and for a fuller and thus more accurate picture, it is recommended that a copy of the report is purchased at £14.50 from Chancery Lane.

Summary

- As at 31st July 1990 there were 67,425 solicitors on the Roll. Of these seventy-six per cent were men and twenty-four per cent women.
- There were 54,734 solicitors holding a current practising certificate entitling them to act as a solicitor. Of these seventy-seven per cent were men and twenty-three per cent were women.
- Of the 54,734 solicitors holding a current practising certificate, 46,652 (eighty-five per cent) were in private practice and seventy-eight per cent of these were men and twenty-two per cent women.
- Apart from private practice, three other significant areas of employment for solicitors holding a practising certificate were local government, commerce and industry and the Crown Prosecution Service (CPS) employing 2,234, 2,177 and 1,100 solicitors respectively (representing ten per cent of solicitors holding a practising certificate).
- At 31st July 1990 there were 12,578 separate organizations employing solicitors in England and Wales of which 10,272 were private practice solicitors' firms. Other organizations employing solicitors included local government, commerce and industry and the Crown Prosecution Service.
- Just over half of the 10,272 solicitors' firms in private practice were based in the South East of England at 31st July 1990, with a quarter of all firms being based in London.

- The gross fees, or turnover to the profession for the year to 31st March 1989 was £3,796 million, an increase of twent-two per cent on the previous year. Provisional figures available for the year to 31st March 1990, show a further increase with gross fees estimated to be about £4,474 million. This represented an increase of about eighteen per cent on 1988-89.
- Average gross fees per fee-earner rose to £56,800 in 1988-89 an increase of fifteen per cent on the previous year. The provisional figure for 1989-90 suggests that average gross fees per fee-earner will have increased to £64,000 in 1989-90, an increase of about thirteen per cent on 1989-90.
- For the year 1st April 1989 to 31st March 1990, total legal aid payments to solicitors amounted to £486.4 million, or 10.9 per cent of the total estimated turnover of solicitors in private practice.
- In 1989-90 the proportion of transfers into the profession doubled with overseas solicitors, barristers and Scottish and Northern Irish solicitors representing sixteen per cent (509) of the 3,729 new solicitors admitted to the Roll.

Solicitors on the Roll 1990

At 31st July 1990, the total number of names on the Roll was 67,425. Women now represent twenty-four per cent of all solicitors on the Roll. (1989: 21.4 per cent).

Solicitors on the Roll with and without practising certificates by sex as at 31st July 1990

With practising certificates	*Number*	*% with certificate*	*% on Roll*
Men	42,051	(76.8%)	62.4%
Women	12,683	(23.2%)	18.8%
Total	54,734	(100.0%)	81.2%
Without practising certificates	*Number*	*% without certificate*	
Men	9,129	(71.9%)	13.5%
Women	3,540	(27.9%)	5.3%
Sex unknown	22	(0.2%)	0.0%
Total	12,691	(100.0%)	18.8%
Total solicitors on the Roll	**67,425**		**100.0%**

Practising certificate holders

The total number of solicitors holding practising certificates on 31st July 1990 was 54,734. Just over eighty-one per cent of solicitors on the Roll hold practising certificates and twenty-three per cent of these are women. A detailed breakdown of the types of employment of practising certificate holders is given below.

Practising certificate holders category of employment as at 31st July 1990 (and non practising certificate holders category of employment where known)

Category of Employment	Total	Men	Women	(No PC*)
Private practice	46,652	36,346	10,306	(1,710)
Local government	2,234	1,586	648	(94)
Commerce/industry	2,177	1,662	515	(217)
Crown Prosecution Service (CPS)	1,100	726	374	(7)
Solicitors abroad	355	273	82	(1,363)
Locum	312	162	150	(25)
National undertaking	227	179	48	(11)
Retired	222	202	20	(1,705)
Clerk/Assistant clerk to Justices	201	168	33	(36)
Law Centre/Citizens Advice Bureau	86	39	47	(0)
Legal Aid Board	73	48	25	(1)
Law Society staff	60	27	33	(5)
Government service	54	39	15	(236)
Not in active practice	40	17	23	(35)
Agent CPS	30	14	16	(2)
Academic	17	12	5	(102)
Other/unknown	894	544	350	(7,142)
Total	54,734	42,051	12,683	(12,691)

* Solicitors not holding a practising certificate at 31st July 1990, but who have indicated their type of employment on annual enrolment or on their last practising certificate before ceasing to practice.

Solicitors' employment

At 31st July 1990 there were 12,653 separate organizations employing solicitors and 10,272 firms in England and Wales in existence. It should be noted that the number of firms in existence changes regularly as a result of mergers, splits, takeovers, etc. These firms were located with 15,551 offices, although the vast majority 7,759 or seventy-six per cent have only one office.

Numbers of organizations employing solicitors by type of business

Type of Business	Head offices England & Wales	Overseas	Branch offices England & Wales	Overseas
Private practice	10,272	46	5,279	156
Local authority	431	0	39	0
Commerce & industry	683	12	136	9
National undertaking	11	0	19	0
Government service	48	2	26	0
Crown Prosecution Service	36	0	95	0
Other/unknown	1,097	15	261	7
Total	12,578	75	5,855	172

Number of firms in private practice at March 1988, 1989 and 1990

Area	1988	1989	% change on 1988	Provisional 1990 figures
A: The North	3,545	3,491	–1.5%	3,397
B: The South	2,554	2,556	+0.1%	2,515
C: London	2,117	2,123	+0.3%	2,014
Non-returns*				279
Total	8,216	8,170	–0.6%	8,205

* The figures for 1990 are provisional since 279 firms (3.4 per cent) had not submitted an annual return to LIB at the time of publication of this report.

The table following shows the changes in the size of firms. It is plain that the number of large firms is increasing.

Sizes of firms in private practice at March 1988, 1989 and 1990

Size of firm (by number of principals)	Number of firms 1988	1989	% Change	Provisional 1990 figures
1	3,075	3,035	−1.3%	2,902
2–4	3,595	3,560	−1.0%	3,459
5–10	1,179	1,180	+0.1%	1,168
11+	367	395	+7.6%	397
Non-returns*				279
Total	8,216	8,170	−0.6%	8,205

* The figures for 1990 are provisional since 279 firms (3.4 per cent) had not submitted an annual return to LIB at the time of publication of this report.

Private practice firms staffing as at about 31st March 1989 by size and region

It can be seen that distribution of solicitors is biased toward London, with little sign of significant change in the profession's general distribution.

Size of firm (ie number of principals)	No of firms	No of principals	Asst sols.	Other fee- earners	Admin staff	% Asst sols.	Non sol staff per sol
London							
1	857	857	346	643	2,214	29%	2.4
2–4	862	2,228	865	1,412	5,970	28%	2.4
5–10	250	1,675	835	1,269	5,074	33%	2.5
11+	154	4,309	5,249	4,303	16,741	55%	2.2
Total	2,123	9,069	7,295	7,627	29,999	45%	2.3
South							
1	985	985	318	775	3,296	24%	3.1
2–4	1,048	2,754	928	2,172	9,475	25%	3.2
5–10	404	2,727	1,108	2,273	9,976	29%	3.2
11+	119	1,977	1,146	1,944	8,055	37%	3.2
Total	2,556	8,443	3,500	7,164	30,802	29%	3.2
North							
1	1,193	1,193	446	860	4,310	27%	3.2
2–4	1,650	4,381	1,464	2,691	14,143	25%	2.9
5–10	526	3,430	1,320	2,443	11,821	28%	3.0
11+	122	2,162	1,478	1,902	8,537	41%	2.9
Total	3,491	11,166	4,708	7,896	38,811	30%	2.9
England & Wales							
Total	8,170	28,678	15,503	22,687	99,612	35%	2.8

Gross fees

Gross fees per principal includes principals who work part-time, so the gross fees per principal represent a minimum figure. Gross fees represent turnover within the profession, rather than income or profit. All overheads, including salaries, must be met out of gross fees. Without a knowledge of the level of these overheads it is not possible to establish the level of earnings of the profession.

Gross fees of firms for 1987-88, 1988-89 and 1989-90

	Gross fees £ million (% increase on previous year)		
Area	1987-88	1988-89	Provisional figures for 1989-90
A: The North	867	1,034 (19%)	1,196
B: The South	770	931 (21%)	1,009
C: London	1,462	1,831 (25%)	2,207
Non-returns*			62
Total	3,099	3,796 (22%)	4,474 (18%)

* The figures for 1990 are provisional since 279 firms (3.4 per cent) had not submitted an annual return to LIB at the time of publication of this report. Last year these firms accounted for £62 million gross fees.

Gross fees for the profession for the year to 31st March 1989 increased nationally by twenty-two per cent on the previous year.

Gross fees per fee-earner* in private practice for the years 1987-88, 1988-89 and provisional figures for 1989-90

Area	1987-88 £'000	1988-89 £'000	Provisional figure for 1989-90 £'000
A: The North	39.1	43.1 (10%)	
B: The South	42.2	48.7 (15%)	
C: London	65.0	77.0 (18%)	
National average	49.2	56.8 (15%)	64.0 (13%)

* Fee earners include solicitors as well as other fee earning staff.

The work of the profession

Indicator	1987	1988	1989	% change on 1988
Total appeals, all courts (Judicial Statistics)	12,551	12,155	11,351	–6.6%
High Court: Proceedings commenced				
Chancery Division	22,868	27,054	30,813	+13.9%
Queen's Bench Division	228,687	235,003	288,287	+22.6%
Family Division:				
Probate	227,682	234,475	231,883	–1.1%
Wardship	–	3,704	4,327	+16.8%
County court:				
Proceedings commenced	2,375,431	2,285,125	2,615,508	+14.5%
Crown court, disposals:				
Committals for trial	96,197	104,773	101,232	–3.4%
Committals for sentence	7,867	8,485	8,267	–2.6%
Appeals	17,053	15,849	16,860	+6.4%
Days sat by judges and registrars	171,926	179,549	182,957	+1.9%

Sources: Lord Chancellor's Department Judicial Statistics Annual Report 1989, Cm 1154 HMSO

Part IV
The qualified career

Legal careers – a general overview

KATRINA SMITH

Katrina Smith is a Consultant with Michael Page Legal, a division of Michael Page Group PLC. She is a qualified solicitor, having served her articles with Dibb Jupton Broomhead in Leeds. Seeking a more commercial role, she joined the Leeds office of Michael Page Legal to coordinate recruitment in Yorkshire, and has recently taken over responsibility for legal recruitment throughout the North of England.

Once you have made the decision to become a lawyer, the next step is to decide whether you wish to practice as a barrister or as a solicitor. Qualifying as a barrister is often viewed as easier than becoming a solicitor, since the examinations are more straightforward and the actual 'training' process is shorter. Once qualified, a solicitor can have a very stable career. A recently admitted barrister still has a number of problems to overcome. The competition for places in chambers is fierce and once a seat has been found, a young barrister without a practice will find work scarce and often of poor quality.

With the government's proposals for multidisciplinary partnerships, more barristers are now requalifying as solicitors and moving into private practice. However, a career at the Bar can be exciting and rewarding, though it is essential to recognize the pitfalls at an early stage and to make your decision accordingly.

The majority of people entering the profession become solicitors, which provides a great variety of experience and many different areas of specialization.

Specializations

As the legal profession develops and diversifies there is a very definite movement towards career specialization.

More recently, with the growth in solicitors' firms and the competition for good quality work, there has emerged a need for lawyers with experience in certain fields. For example, three to five years ago a newly qualified solicitor was expected to specialize in company work; today he or she would need to concentrate on just one area such as corporate finance, or merger and acquisition work, to enable the firm to provide the client with a good and competitive service. There is no doubt that the more specialized the experience, the more in demand your skills as a solicitor will be. Therefore, it is essential that, if you wish to specialize early in your career, you ensure that you gain the relevant experience in articles or soon thereafter.

The most specialized and fast developing areas of law include planning law, intellectual property, corporate finance, taxation, criminal litigation, construction, private client, insolvency and general practice, which is indeed a specialism in itself.

Industry

In recent years, the growth in commerce and industry, particularly in the South of England, has brought about the role of the in-house lawyer. This has meant that an increasing number of barristers and solicitors have left private practice to pursue a career in industry. Many have moved to gain more on-line commercial experience and others have chosen this career path because it offers a completely different approach to private practice.

In private practice, a solicitor will have a large number of clients and will divide time between them, advising on many aspects of law. In industry, however, a lawyer has just one client, the company itself, and time is spent providing legal advice to the board.

Career progression within practice is very clear, through trainee solicitor, assistant solicitor, associate, salaried partner to equity partner. In industry, career progression does not follow any typical plan. Therefore, a lawyer may progress from a junior in the legal department through to management, or possibly may change direction to become company secretary eventually to secure a position on the board.

One other slight difference between private practice and industry is evidenced in remuneration levels. Previously, salaries in practice were higher than in industry. Recently, however, there has been a levelling off and salaries, although still competitive, are now comparable and industrial appointments often include benefits such as a car or a subsidized mortgage. However, unless a board position or other senior post is obtained, there is a financial ceiling in industry and a solicitor in practice who achieves partnership status will quickly overtake his industrial counterpart.

A barrister in practice is self-employed. In industry he is employed by the company which not only prevents him from having his own practice but which also restricts his rights of audience.

There are many industrial sectors to consider such as energy, retail, manufacturing, engineering, banking and financial services. Again, specialization and experience are of paramount importance. Relevant specializations for industry are company/commercial, taxation, corporate finance and property. If you eventually seek a career in industry it is useful to think ahead and to tailor your experience towards the future.

Careers outside practice or industry

As a qualified lawyer there are a large number of options available and some examples are as follows:

Local government
This offers wide experience in many aspects of local government law including planning, childcare, highways and housing. Salaries are good, but again have a finite level, and the transition from local government to private practice is often difficult. However, good planning or building experience is very much in demand in private practice and will assist any move.

The magistrates' court
Here, a solicitor will gain exposure to all aspects of magistrates' court procedure and at a senior level will adopt the role of the magistrate's clerk, providing advice to the magistrates on all aspects of law.

The Crown Prosecution Service
Established by the judiciary, this service provides excellent advocacy and criminal litigation experience to those wishing to specialize in this field. The service is made up of both barristers and solicitors, who act on a day-to-day basis in representing the Crown in the criminal courts.

The forces
The army, the navy and the RAF all recruit solicitors with good advocacy experience to work at home or abroad, largely handling court martial and criminal defence work. The normal selection procedures are adopted and, in the army, a lawyer will enter service at the rank of Captain.

Law centres

Law centres deal directly with the community providing legal advice for those without access to a solicitor. Handling mainly legal aid work, the function of a law centre is similar to the citizens advice bureau, except it employs qualified staff and the CAB consists largely of unqualified volunteers.

For lawyers who are committed to a career in the profession, there are such a variety of different options available that anyone should be able to find a niche to match their own character, aspirations and ambitions. Similarly, the lawyer who no longer wishes to pursue a career in the law can use his or her qualification as a stepping stone to other areas such as legal recruitment, business development or lecturing.

With industry and private practice still expanding and diversifying, and the prospects of 1992's European market fast approaching, the future of the legal profession is looking better than ever.

A serious business

JONATHAN DENNY

Jonathan Denny is full-time Managing Partner at Cripps Harries Hall, a progressive firm of solicitors rated in the top four in the South East, structured and managed on business principles. He argues that, for some trainees, a career as a solicitor can now offer the challenges and rewards of business as well as those of the law.

There is a deadpan little phrase which appears at the bottom of advertisements extolling the success of investment funds in sending their investors' cash forth to multiply. It runs, 'Past performance cannot guarantee a future performance' – or something like that.

The moral is that whatever the fund you invest in may look like today, the picture may be very different in five, ten or twenty years' time. It is a useful text to bear in mind for those who are about to invest their career prospects in a particular firm. The firm of solicitors that you join today will be very different from the business that you end up running in the twenty-first century.

I am picking my words carefully here. The whole legal profession is undergoing rapid change. Solicitors have been thrust by economic and legislative changes into the business of selling legal services. The structure of today's solicitors partnership is, however, based on the Partnership Act which gives each and every partner the rights and responsibilities for the management of their firm – a democratic but dangerously unwieldy structure for late twentieth century business conditions.

The Bar's structure, of course, based on a long tradition of single practitioners, is likely to undergo more dramatic and obvious change. For solicitors, the changes will be more gradual and subtle at first, but just as far reaching.

The trainee solicitors of today can expect to see huge changes not only in the nature of the 'firm' which they join, but also in the role that they will play within it during their careers. The position of a trainee solicitor joining a firm is now much closer than ever before to the position of the management trainee joining a company.

In the days when they were called articled clerks, trainee solicitors could look forward to progression through the stages of assistant solicitor, associate, partner and – perhaps just for a year or two – senior partner. That ladder of seniority still exists but a number of managerial posts have made their appearance up and down it: managing partner, marketing partner, finance partner, recruitment partner. There are, however, still very few firms who have people in all these positions, and few where these posts are filled on a full-time basis.

Some firms which thought they should make management appointments have attempted a management halfway house. Rather than have the partners manage as a body, specific appointments have been given to people who were felt not to be integral to the success of the firm. The trend is increasingly to employ non-legally trained professionals, but the amateur approach lingers on in more places than it ought.

The instinctive unwillingness among some firms to allow fee-earners to use their time on management functions rather than client business has often been a barrier to a more professional attitude to management. Among progressive – and successful – firms, however, there is explicit recognition that effective management of resources is the crucial factor in a healthy bottom line, and that lawyers need to become confident in management techniques.

The implications are that the young assistant solicitor of tomorrow with aptitude for the work, might take on specific responsibility for the firm's marketing strategy, working in tandem with (or replacing) a marketing professional. It is quite possible that experience of a management post such as marketing will become a recognized ingredient of the high flyer's career mix. Equally, such a pattern could provide an alternative career option, allowing a move out of the legal side of the business altogether.

Many lawyers, most in fact, will probably want to stay with the law as a profession. Even so, with direct management experience they will have a much better understanding of the business culture from which their clients come.

The key word in all this is 'management'. Many firms now claim to have a managing partner, but few have allowed that partner to relinquish his client duties, with the result that the management function is all too often part-time and second best. The more progressive firm will usually have a full-time managing partner working through a structure which devolves management responsibility as far down the line as possible, and divides the firm into profit centres.

This means that even the newest trainee will be exposed to an atmosphere of basic management problem-solving and taking business decisions. Later on in his or her career, the partner can be expected to take a seat on the firm's executive board, the 'cabinet' which decides general policy. This does not mean that the other partners have lost control or no longer matter. But only the most major decisions on the partnership or strategic direction of the firm tend nowadays to be taken by the partners, meeting as a whole.

The devolution of responsibility means that today's trainees will encounter management responsibility much earlier than ever before. Immediately they will be aware not only of the necessity to make productive use of time on client work – the basis of the firm's profitability – but also of the business decisions which need to be taken: hiring; firing; borrowing; and investing.

Further up the ladder there is a good chance that the partner of tomorrow will be responsible for the performance and profitability of his or her own unit within the firm. At some stage he or she may be involved in merger talks. By the time he gets to be managing partner, he may even be discussing the incorporation or flotation of the partnership on the Unlisted Securities Market!

The irony of all this is that the lawyer in a firm may get much more direct management experience than his or her colleagues working in-house in industry. The in-house lawyer does of course get the opportunity to move into mainstream management, but the partner in the firm is already there.

If the newly qualified solicitor is likely to become rapidly involved in management situations, especially in the faster moving medium-sized firm, is the training he or she receives adequate? As things stand at present, the answer must almost certainly be 'no'. Business and management training for lawyers should ideally start at law school, although few taking Law Society Finals would welcome another subject and another paper.

The best place for more specific training is the firm, once the trainees have found their feet as solicitors, something we make a point of at Cripps Harries Hall. But in today's climate, in the well run solicitors office, the trainee will be aware of the commercial culture right from the word go. We live in tough – but interesting – times.

Specialization within a law firm

JOHN BOARDMAN

John Boardman is a Partner at Alexander Tatham, which is a member of
Eversheds, the first national law firm with a truly nationwide network of
offices. Having completed his articles at the firm, he is now Head of the
Corporate Department at Alexander Tatham as well as being Chairman of the
National Groups across Eversheds, which cover areas of law and different
industries.

Eversheds, which is used as an illustration to show what a commercial firm's
departments cover, has offices in major commercial centres in England and
Wales. The firm has 1600 people, including 182 partners, and offers clients
the breadth and depth of commercial legal advice normally only associated
with a London firm.

Eversheds' services are provided to clients through the following
departments, and you would normally expect to find some or all of these
departments in a typical commercial law firm:

Corporate

Corporate finance covers many kinds of commercial and financial transactions,
including company formations, management buy-outs take-overs, mergers,
reconstructions and joint ventures. In addition, advice on financing such
transactions is given.

We have experience in many aspects of stock exchange work and as well
as acting for quoted companies, Eversheds advises merchant banks, brokers
and clients wishing to bring companies to the Stock Exchange.

Commercial

Very often corporate and commercial departments are combined, and
certainly they work closely together. In the case of Eversheds' commercial
departments, these cover commercial agreements, franchising, distribution

and agency agreements, licensing (both in the UK and overseas) and patents, copyright and other aspects of intellectual property.

Intellectual property is a rapidly expanding area of law advice, and individuals within the group are specializing further into computer contracts and the specialisms of a variety of industry sectors.

Property

We advise on all aspects of freehold and leasehold transactions relating to all types of commercial property through England and Wales as well as the property aspects of company take-overs, mergers and reconstructions.

Housing departments, project funding and contract negotiation are also dealt with by this department.

Planning

In some firms this department comes under the property department, as in the case of Eversheds. The work deals with planning queries on factories and housing and much time is spent relating to planning appeals.

Litigation

We handle a wide range of matters from the substantial commercial claims in dispute which involve High Court litigation to the smaller cases dealt with by the County Court. Our litigation service also extends to contract and building disputes.

Eversheds is also one of the leaders in both environmental law and fraud protection, both of which have a strong litigation element.

Employment

The employment group advises on the complete range of employment law, from unfair dismissal to race relations. Debt recovery, which includes building society mortgage arrears and debt collection, is playing an increasingly important role with the development of the appropriate computerized systems to assist clients.

Insolvency

Insolvency departments are another area of specialist law, advising companies on receiverships, liquidations, administrations and the personal liabilities of directors who may be responsible for wrongful trading.

European law

While European law now affects all UK clients, many firms, including Eversheds, have specialists in touch with Brussels and advising on the effects of latest EC law. Particularly relevant at present is advising companies on competition law and ensuring that standard contracts and documentation are updated in line with EC law.

Private client

In the case of Eversheds, the private client departments offer a comprehensive advisory service covering all aspects of setting up and administering trusts, personal taxation and planning pensions, wills and probate.

Commercial firms differ in what their private client departments offer, and some will split into tax and trust departments and private client departments which may deal with the variety of problems of individuals, including domestic conveyancing, matrimonial problems, road traffic work and small claims.

Criminal

Eversheds as a firm concentrates on commercial rather than the criminal aspects of law. However, most commercial firms will deal with 'white collar' crimes such as fraud. In those firms which have strong criminal departments, the work covers defending all types of criminal prosecution, including legal aid work.

Industry specializations

An understanding of the individual problems of different industries has led Eversheds to set up national groups of lawyers who have in-depth knowledge of particular industries across a broad range of legal areas. Examples are brewing, construction, shipping and banking groups. In these cases a team of lawyers from different departments will advise a client calling on the relevant legal area lawyer and an industry specialist.

The above gives an outline of the typical departments you can expect to find in a commercial law firm, and some of the newer areas of specialization which can be found in the larger firms, such as environment, fraud and European law.

Company and commercial law

CHRISTOPHER DUNN

Slater Heelis was founded in 1773 and is now one of the leading firms of solicitors in the North West. The firm has an extensive commercial practice with departments covering company/commercial, banking and insolvency, litigation, property and probate and trust work. Christopher Dunn is a Partner in the Company and Commercial Department.

'Company and commercial law' is a very wide area but the distinctive thing about the work of a company commercial department is that it involves advice to business clients about business matters.

At my firm this means that the solicitors in the department see a number of different types of client ranging from large structured organizations such as clearing and merchant banks, listed PLCs and the UK subsidiaries of multinationals to medium sized and old established family businesses and new start-ups, perhaps the result of a management buyout.

The work for the clients is as varied as the clients themselves so that we may become involved in discussing anything from engineering to computers, sports goods to management consultancy and textiles to property development. When a client rings with a new matter, it may be any one of a number of things: a proposed acquisition of a business from a receiver on very tight time constraints; a confidentiality agreement before talks begin with a customer concerning a new product; or a problem between directors and shareholders where the client, who believed he had a partnership with his colleagues, now fears that he is being squeezed out.

The largest firms of solicitors frequently divide mainstream company commercial work at least into 'corporate finance and transactional work' and 'commercial work'.

As the phrase suggests, corporate finance or transactional work tends to be focused on a particular business arrangement. We may be acting on behalf of a company or a sponsoring institution, on a stock exchange listing or public issue, advising about and putting into effect a company reorganization, acquisition or disposal, acting for one of the parties to a management buyout, or offering advice about and preparing an agreement for a joint venture or a venture capital arrangement.

'Public company' transactions require a very high level of disclosure to the public together with strict compliance with the Regulations of the Stock Exchange and/or the Code on Take Overs and Mergers ('the Yellow Book' and 'the Blue Book') in addition to statutory and common law requirements. As solicitors acting we attend drafting meetings with clients, merchant banks, accountants and brokers, prepare offer documentation, circulars and listing particulars and detailed verification notes intended to confirm the accuracy of any statements made in those documents.

In a transaction involving a private company we take instructions, draft documents and negotiate with the other party's solicitors. The aim is to establish a working relationship with everyone involved in order to progress the transaction. Many clients only take part in such a transaction once in a lifetime and rely heavily on professional advisers.

Market uncertainty has caused some reduction in stock exchange related work in the last three years, but there has been an increase in merger and acquisition activity (both in relation to listed and private companies) which has compensated for this. We have found that trade sales and MBOs offer alternatives for shareholders seeking to realize their investment despite the general climate.

'Commercial work' is primarily contract based and covers the whole spectrum of commercial agreements – agency and distribution agreements, computer contracts, franchising arrangements and terms and conditions of trading being a few examples. We may be asked to prepare standard documents such as conditions of sale which do not relate specifically to any single transaction but which may be used by the client on numerous occasions in the sale of products worth millions of pounds. This requires an understanding of the way in which the business of that client operates and an ability to prepare detailed documentation without the stimulus of another solicitor considering the draft for 'the other side'. We may also be asked to advise a client about one particular contract (such as a distributorship agreement) and this may well involve the familiar challenges of negotiation and drafting under time pressure.

The classification of two types of work is to some extent both artificial and incomplete as the company commercial department will become involved in other types of work, such as advising banks in relation to facility documentation or on the financial assistance aspect of a takeover, providing support for the insolvency department in the sale of companies and assets by administrative receivers and liquidators, and liaising with the litigation department. The liaison with the litigation department is particularly fruitful and interesting where the court is being asked to decide a point of company law; in such a case the litigation department will seek advice as the case proceeds (sometimes to the Court of Appeal or House of Lords) on the various arguments which are being put forward.

The above outline should give some indication of the characteristics required by the ideal practitioner of company commercial law. This paragon must not only possess legal ability but also needs commercial awareness and common sense, sensitivity to the needs of the client, and communicating and negotiating skills. It is necessary to reconcile the demands of urgency and caution and at all times to be able to 'see the woods for the trees' – that is to remain keenly aware of the client's aims and of those elements of the transaction which are essential whilst not forgetting every legal implication.

Not only must the company commercial lawyer have all these skills, but it is also vitally important that he or she can work well as part of a team with clients, with other professional advisers and with the property, employment, tax and other company solicitors in the firm working on a particular transaction. Successful teamwork ensures that the job is well done and also helps to develop high morale and a good atmosphere within a firm. Slater Heelis has doubled the number of its fee earners in the last three years but we have consciously sought to retain friendliness and cooperation within a hardworking professional environment.

Company and commercial law involves long hours and pressure but it carries with it considerable rewards. The satisfaction of achieving difficult objectives for a client, the satisfaction of working as part of a high quality team and the satisfaction of seeing an enormous amount of paperwork fit together at last!

'If you miss I'll sue for personal injury.'

Practising in planning law

LEWIS A DENTON

Lewis A Denton is a Senior Planning Lawyer in the Property Department at Davies Wallis Foyster, a large commercial law firm with offices in Liverpool, Manchester and Blackburn. He is a solicitor who specialized in planning and related areas in local government for over sixteen years, before moving to his present position.

Although the majority of specialist planning lawyers are still to be found in local government, and a handful have even joined the civil service as members of the Capital Planning Inspectorate, over the last few years there has been an enormous growth in the number of planning lawyers in private practice. This has resulted from an increasing awareness by clients of the financial consequences of planning decisions, the need for specialist advice, and a rapid growth in the size of many commercial firms of lawyers which enabled them to support specialists in this field. It still remains true, however, that most planning lawyers gained their initial experience within local government. The subject has a reputation for complexity but the basic principles can be assimilated by newcomers quite rapidly.

The attraction of planning law is that, although it is a specialized field, it covers a wide span of human activity, and much of the work is high profile. Planning is concerned with the control of development of land, and the issues involved in deciding whether or not planning permission should be granted for a particular development can be complex and varied. The lengthy public inquiries into major road schemes and nuclear power station proposals for example, are well known and often make headline news. Even an application or appeal involving a proposed town centre development of shops and offices includes an assessment of the impact on the commercial viability of existing shops, the effect of projected traffic growth on the road system and those living nearby, the desirability of generating new employment and other issues. The planning lawyer must be able to take on board all these issues and have some understanding of them, even though he or she will be working with specialists in those fields.

Because the planning process often involves balancing the needs of the community at large against the interests or wishes of those who propose to develop land, the process is rarely 'black and white', and issues are often finely balanced. A planning lawyer is almost invariably working with a team of specialist professionals in other fields, such as planners, highway engineers, ecologists and noise consultants, and is often cast in the role of coordinator of a multi-disciplinary team. Planning practice therefore tends to suit those who thrive on cooperation and team work. The local government lawyer will be working principally with other professionals within the same authority or another body, eg the regional water supply company, whereas in private practice he or she will often advise the client on the particular consultants thought necessary to present the case in the best possible way, and work with the resulting team. In both cases, there is often considerable contact with councillors, local amenity societies and members of the public, many of whom have strong views about what should or should not happen in their locality. The planning lawyer therefore also needs the diplomatic skills to deal with what can sometimes become a very heated situation.

At present, the prospects for planning lawyers are good. At times of fast economic growth developments of land usually proceeds at a rapid pace, and therefore generates a variety and volume of work. Even when there is an economic downturn, the skills of a planning lawyer may be even more in demand as house builders or investment companies seek to maximize the development potential of some of their less desirable sites. It should not be forgotten that planning is often a long-term process, and the scene is set by structure and local plans (and in metropolitan areas by Unitary Development Plans) to which clients have a right to object. Central government is now insisting on comprehensive local plan coverages, and astute land owners and developers will wish to be advised on how these plans will affect their position, sometimes years ahead of actual development taking place.

Recent central government initiatives are also likely to produce additional work for planning lawyers. Due to the advent of Urban Development Corporations, with powers of compulsory purchase, and increased spending on new roads, the planning lawyer is becoming increasingly involved in dealing with compulsory purchase matters. No-one can fail to have noticed the renewed interest in environmental and 'green' issues, many of which relate to the development of land. At the time of writing, an Environmental Protection Bill is going through parliament. There is already a tendency for planning lawyers to be involved in issues of environmental law, and there is little doubt that this promises to be a major growth area for lawyers who have a grasp of the issues involved. Professionally, the prospects are very exciting.

A career in planning law is therefore something which presents a stimulating intellectual challenge, as a grasp of many issues other than law is required, there is the opportunity to use advocacy skills at public inquiries, and there is the exciting prospect of continued expansion into related areas of environmental law.

Criminal law

DAVID SAVAGE

David Savage, who was admitted as a solicitor in 1963, is a Partner in the firm of Foster Savage and Gordon of Farnborough in Hampshire. He is a past President of the Hampshire Incorporated Law Society, and currently serves as a member of the Law Society's Criminal Law Committee. His firm has a reputation for advocacy in the criminal and civil courts.

Practitioners are attracted to work in the criminal courts for a number of reasons. The problem has always been to retain experienced advocates, who in later years are reluctant to undertake legal aid work, because of the poor rewards.

We live in a changing society. Values, ideals and aspirations are subject to continuous re-appraisal. It is against this background that the rule of law and the rights of the individual must be upheld. The clamour to give the police wider powers to fight crime is constant. But what of individual rights? The defence solicitor, especially the duty solicitor on call twenty-four hours a day, is as much involved in the fight against crime as anyone else.

Those embarking upon a career in the criminal law, whether it be the Crown Prosecution Service, or as a private practitioner, can look forward to a stimulating career, in which one must never sacrifice or compromise one's independence. Whatever proposals are brought forward for franchising legal services, the right of the individual to select his own advocate must remain. It is this independence which will preserve confidence in our legal system.

Change is our ally. The publication of the Lord Chancellor's proposals for the reform of the legal profession turned the spotlight on the future of the criminal practitioner, with proposals to widen rights of audience in the higher courts and especially in the crown court. Unfortunately, so much has been written and said about this issue that one is in danger of losing right of the arguments. Most lawyers seem to overlook the fact that solicitors already enjoy considerable rights of audience in the crown courts in some parts of the country, and these rights have existed since time immemorial. Why should these rights not be extended throughout England and Wales? Is not the client entitled to have the advocate of his choice?

If the rights of audience in the criminal courts are to be extended, then practitioners embarking upon a career as a criminal law specialist will have to undergo further training before appearing in the higher courts. The technique and style of advocacy is different. Procedural points and technicalities will have to be learnt and mastered. For those with the motivation, the opportunities will open up a distinct career structure. Promotion will become most frequent from the ranks of solicitors, although it may be some years before a solicitor is appointed the first High Court Judge.

Most criminal work is publicly funded. Each year the pay round is fraught with difficulty. The Lord Chancellor's Department is pressurized by the Treasury to contain expenditure, and the profession seems fortunate if it secures an increase in pay rates which keeps abreast of inflation. Whilst pay is not the most important criterion for a criminal practitioner (job satisfaction is far more so) it is impossible to provide a service with constantly rising overheads. Is it not time to take a fundamental look at the cost of criminal legal aid? Does every aspect of the case have to be handled by an experienced lawyer in open court? Expense and time could be saved if committee proceedings were abolished. Why should applications for advanced disclosure be dealt with in open court? Could not some adjournments and remands (often administrative matters) be dealt with by the clerk, subject to a right of appeal? Changes should be made to make the courts more efficient and cost conscious. Fixed fees for criminal work will be introduced, and only the most efficient firms will be able to afford to undertake legal aid work.

Over the years I have defended the 'indefensible' and excused the 'inexcusable'. Human behaviour has never ceased to amaze me. That is what makes the job so worthwhile.

Working with property

JOHN REDMOND

John Redmond joined Laytons in 1978 to assist in opening the firm's Bristol office. As Litigation Partner of the new office, he gradually concentrated more and more on the construction industry. He now manages this work for the firm's Southern Region, with offices in London, Surrey and Bristol.

Whilst the political debate continues about whether recession struck in 1989, 1990 or not at all, there has been little debate in the construction industry. Builders know when times are hard. When the industry suffers, the professions that serve the industry suffer too, or do they?

Lawyers who devote themselves to construction contract litigation are of course busy when the industry is busy. If there are not enough bricklayers to go round, progress on building sites falls behind. If there are not enough experienced site managers, sites are not properly managed. Claims result, as building contracts fall further and further into delay, and everyone blames everyone else.

But when times are slack, building contractors seek to recover every penny of entitlement under their contracts and need to resist vigorously any spurious claims by sub-contractors and suppliers. Some contractors will even price their tenders low in the belief that their energetic lawyers will be able to extract enough through claims to make a profit on the deal. And so the construction litigation practice is busy again.

The quiet time is the middle period, when there is plenty of work to go round, but also adequate labour and material supply. Equilibrium. No-one wants or needs to sue or arbitrate, and legal bills go down fast.

Unfortunately for the industry, the middle period has been squeezed out completely by the shortening of the cycle. Boom gives way to bust and reverts to boom again so fast that equilibrium is never achieved. The building litigator finds that he is still heavily involved in boom litigation when the bust litigation pours in through the door.

Anyone who reads the legal press will be aware of the growth of 'specialist' construction litigation departments in recent years. Such departments used to be a feature of the Central London firms, but are now appearing in provincial commercial firms as well.

The growth of litigation may explain the growth in the number of solicitors in the field, but why the sudden development outside London? This is partly due to economies, and partly due to the effect of several years marketing efforts by a few established provincial construction practices.

Times being hard, builders need to think about how much their lawyers are costing them. A professional's charging rate, calculated to recover a proper share of a practice's overheads, will always boggle the mind of a builder used to hourly charging of skilled site labour. But the enormous expense of operating in Central London can mean that the extraordinarily high cost of a solicitor based in a provincial city is doubled if the solicitor is based there. Construction litigation work is hour intensive. Very many hours will be spent in litigating even a moderate sized claim, and the cost is prohibitive.

Clearly, there could be no justification in selecting a provincial lawyer at half the London charging rate if he/she was going to take three times as long to do the job, and/or make a complete mess of it. If though, the contractor believes that the service and expertise are as good, the economy will be attractive.

The expertise has always been available but it used to take some finding. Lights are no longer hidden under bushels, and lawyers who practice in relatively esoteric areas like construction are now able and prepared to say so. Laytons Bristol office is an example.

Laytons had practised in construction law through its Lancashire and London offices for many years. When we opened a Bristol office in 1978, building contract litigation immediately became a principle area of work, with substantial instructions coming from a handful of clients. Growth in the client base was, however, modest. It was not until the restrictions on advertising were relaxed that any conscious attempt was made to market the skills and expertise that had been built up. A quarterly publication *Laytons Building* began to be circulated to clients and contacts such as expert witnesses. Appearances at seminars, some organized by others and some for the firm's own clients, helped to spread the word. More recently an advice and referral service for other solicitors was established, which has attracted some attention from the specialist press.

Meanwhile, the practice continued with the best marketing method of all – the satisfied client. Large construction companies who had thought of

Laytons as their 'local Bristol' solicitor began to refer instructions from further afield. As managers from clients progressed their own careers by moving to other companies, so the practice's reputation expanded. At the end of 1990, six lawyers now handle exclusively construction related work within the Bristol office, whereas only two years before, three lawyers had devoted an average of half their time to it.

The case load includes relatively minor county court litigation for local sub-contractor tradesmen or general builders who are not being paid for their efforts at loft conversion. But most of the work is in the commercial building market, acting for substantial main contractors and 'works package' contractors. Instructions are regularly received from European contractors working in the UK, who find that English building contracts have features that take them by surprise. The clients and the buildings themselves are quite likely to be in Hamburg or Newcastle rather than Bristol. The 'building' may well not be a building at all, but a motorway, a reservoir or even, in one case, a large aquarium fish tank.

No doubt several other provincial practices could tell a similar story, in construction and other specialist fields. The quality, high value work which used to be the exclusive territory of the London 'big name' firms is now regularly coming to those of us out in other commercial centres. As a result, many lawyers who thought that they had to live and work in London in order to deal with work that interested them are moving out too. The quality of the advice available therefore improves further, and there is still more incentive to use the provincial solicitor. These are exciting times, and I am glad I do not work in London.

A career in taxation

SARAH FALK and COLIN HARGREAVES

Sarah Falk and Colin Hargreaves work as Assistant Solicitors in the Corporate Tax Department at Freshfields, a large City firm of solicitors. They both did their articles at Freshfields before qualifying in the tax department. Sarah is four years qualified, Colin is two-and-a-half years qualified.

The tax department at Freshfields is one of the largest tax departments in any firm of solicitors. The department has nine partners, twenty-nine legal staff, eleven trainee solicitors and associated support staff. The work which we handle in the department reflects Freshfields' position as a major City commercial firm, and is concerned principally with corporate and related taxation.

The emphasis is very much on considering and resolving challenging legal points and on the structuring of transactions. Very little of our time is spent in the production of lengthy agreements or other documents, this work being handled principally by other departments in the firm. Nor does the work which we deal with involve preparation of tax computations (which will normally be handled by client's auditors). We have a good deal of contact with tax barristers, and some with Inland Revenue Head Office specialists. The work in a tax department such as ours is probably best suited of all the specializations to a fairly academic approach.

The variety of work available in tax is much greater than you might think. As well as being involved in giving 'pure' tax advice in relation to businesses we tend to get involved at an early stage in structuring takeover and company restructuring, and in all types of financing work, including borrowing on the capital markets and leasing. We work directly for our own clients, and also assist other departments (particularly the company and commercial department) and our overseas offices in transactions of many kinds, often with an increasing international character (reflected in the formation recently of our international tax group).

We also get involved in tax litigation – not generally of the 'non payment' kind – but often involving very large amounts and turning on important legal points.

One of the advantages in working in a department like ours is the way in which information is shared. Tax is a continually developing subject, so it is vital not only to keep well informed of new developments, but also to be able to discuss difficult points with others and be aware of the issues that others are dealing with. This is dealt with both on a formal basis (through a weekly journal) and in other ways, not least through informal discussions.

Although large as *tax* departments go, the tax department is a small department when contrasted with the company/commercial teams in any of the big City firms of solicitors. As a result, members of the department tend to know each other well and there is a strong emphasis on the social side of activities within the department. In addition, the fact that fewer people are involved in City tax work than are involved in City commercial work overall carries the advantage that we tend to know most of our counterparts in the tax departments of other City firms reasonably well.

The work of an intellectual property solicitor

ELIZABETH GIBSON

Lovell White Durrant was formed in May 1988 by the merger of Lovell, White & King and Durrant Piesse, both leading City firms. Lovell White Durrant has established a strong reputation in a wide range of intellectual property work. Elizabeth Gibson served her articles with Lovell White & King and joined the firm's Intellectual Property Department when she qualified as a solicitor in 1977.

The term 'intellectual property' is now much more readily understood than it used to be, both by students of law and the general public. The term refers to the variety of legal rights which can be asserted in respect of what might be described as 'the products of the human intellect'. These rights include patents, copyright and design rights, registered designs, confidential information (or trade secrets), trademarks and service marks, and the right to prevent passing off.

In the past, expertise in these different rights tended to be concentrated in separate pockets of legal knowledge that did not necessarily overlap. A lawyer who knew about trademarks would not necessarily know about patents; licensing of copyright was usually quite separate from infringement actions; trade secrets were considered an offshoot of employment law. The department I first joined in 1977 was a mixture of 'builders and other boffins' expected to deal with construction disputes and 'anything technical'. I had never dealt with this area of the law before, and a degree in English did not seem an obvious advantage in a group where qualifications in engineering or science were the norm. However, I was soon captivated by the legal problems that arose, and the astonishing breadth of subject matter.

The construction side of the group has since gone its separate way, and the 'technical' bias of the work has broadened. The lawyers in our group are now fairly evenly divided between those with scientific qualifications and those without, including many with degrees in subjects other than law. The group now advises on a much wider range of non-contentious matters which might previously have been dealt with by other departments in the firm, including the drafting and negotiation of licences and computer contracts. However, the appealing mixture of the technical and the mundane, the range of clients from struggling inventors to multinational corporations, remains the same. We act in highly technical patent infringement actions between major domestic and foreign corporations. The subject matter can be chemical or pharmaceutical, electronic or mechanical: reflective road signs, suspension systems for cars, polymer baler twine, steroid creams and electronic organs (the musical variety) are some of the products we have dealt with. At the same time equally major corporations may be litigating over the appearance of a tub of baby wipes or a plastic squeezy lemon. Ex-employees of a company may be accused of taking confidential information with them, in the form of computer software or even genetically engineered 'bugs'. An advertising agency or publishing house may suddenly find that their latest campaign or magazine title infringes someone else's trademark. An individual may complain that he has been unfairly injuncted by a cosmetics company for selling counterfeit goods, or seek advice on whether a new idea for a doorbell is patentable.

What kind of person makes a good intellectual property lawyer? In my view, this is a field where knowledge of the law and a meticulous approach to detail are vital. While one must always be aware of the commercial realities of the situation, the protection and enforcement of intellectual property rights are fraught with legal difficulties and the intricacies of the statutes, the significance of a particular word in a licence agreement, may be of fundamental importance. In many cases there is no short cut through the laborious and painstaking work necessary to prepare a copyright or patent infringement case for trial, or to advise on the validity of patents or trademarks about to be licensed or assigned. Yet combined with this is the 'gut feeling' one instinctively acquires from experience. Does an advertising jingle infringe copyright in a well known piece of music? Is the appearance or packaging of a new product going to cause confusion when it appears on the supermarket shelves? Is an extract from a published article 'fair dealing'? The answers to these questions will not be found in the statutes or textbooks. You must make your own judgement as to what a court is likely to say, and in the field of passing off in particular one's own reaction as a housewife or consumer is often as good a guide as any.

Obtaining suitable evidence in support of your case also calls on these different skills. The expert witness in a patent case must be carefully selected and meticulously briefed by a lawyer with sufficient technical knowledge both to understand what the expert is saying and to see any possible flaws in his reasoning. Finding witnesses to give evidence of confusion in a passing off case involves a more subtle approach. Can you find people who do not mind admitting that they have been confused? Will they appear genuine and credible to the judge? Can you persuade them to swear an affidavit or come to court? You must respond to these people in a much more personal way.

You must also be prepared to take urgent action for a client at a moment's notice if the need arises. The 'Anton Piller' order originated in the field of copyright and trade mark infringement to deal with the problem of counterfeiting. As well as meticulous care in preparing the application to the court and ensuring, as tactfully as you can, that your client makes full disclosure of all the relevant facts, a cool head is needed to serve these orders on what may be a frightened, potentially violent or unpredictable defendant. The skills and effort needed to coordinate the exercise of serving the order, searching the defendant's premises, counting and removing what may be several thousand counterfeit articles into a hired van and then to safe custody, as well as advising the defendant of his rights and restraining what may be a somewhat over-enthusiastic team of trainee solicitors, should not be underestimated!

The last few years have seen many changes in intellectual property law – the new Copyright Designs and Patents Act has completely altered protection for industrial articles, and the Trade Marks Act is also soon to be overhauled. The way solicitors and other professionals in the field work together is also changing. The new Patents County Court opened in October 1990, where solicitors and patent agents can present cases on behalf of their clients without the need to instruct a barrister. Proposals to extend solicitors' rights of audience in the High Court are currently being implemented. All this will result in greater opportunities and challenges to the solicitor to provide a complete service for the client, and carry a case through from preparation to presentation in court.

So, be you scientist or arts graduate, litigator or negotiator, draughtsman or would-be advocate, there can be opportunities and rewards in intellectual property for all of you!

Private client work in a large firm

PETER KEMPSTER

Peter Kempster is qualified as both a Solicitor and a Chartered Accountant. He is the Head of the Tax and Trusts Department at Nabarro Nathanson, one of the ten largest firms in the country. As well as handling commercial tax work, the department has a dozen lawyers specializing in private client work.

'Our firm's departments? Well, we have company, property, litigation . . . oh, and private client, of course.' The private client department of a large firm is often regarded as something slightly out of the mainstream. The work is seen as somehow uncommercial, and the lawyers as somewhat of a different breed.

This article looks at the work handled, and the people who do it. First, what is private client work?

The work

In large firms, the private client department generally handles those matters where the client is an individual or a family, rather than a corporation. The work requires knowledge of a wide range of legal topics: property law: 'If I give a half share in my house to my son could he force me to sell the house?'; company law: 'If I put my family company shares into a Jersey trust, who decides how the votes will be cast?'; matrimonial law: 'I won't have to talk to my first husband about all this, will I?'

But the bulk of the work concerns the areas of taxation, trusts and succession. This combination is no coincidence. The private clients of large firms are often wealthy individuals who look to their solicitors for advice on the management and preservation of their wealth for themselves and their descendants. Reducing the incidence of taxation is obviously of prime importance. The trust has always been, and continues to be, one of the most flexible and efficient methods of personal financial planning.

These areas of law are themselves wide-ranging. Take, for example, the international dimension. The legitimate use of offshore tax havens plays a large role in the strategies of private client lawyers so that the work has a

115

considerable foreign legal content. Similarly, the UK tax system contains certain beneficial rules for individuals domiciled abroad; these often necessitate the retention of assets outside the UK so that private client lawyers are proficient in the subject of private international law. Moreover, the preparation of wills and the administration of probate usually involves large and complex estates, often with assets in several foreign jurisdictions.

Private client lawyers are also expected to advise on charity law. Questions which arise range from an existing educational charity asking whether the provision of a cricket pitch could be regarded as charitable, to an individual enquiring whether he can establish his own charitable trust for the benefit of children with leukaemia.

As if all this were not enough, because private client lawyers have an expertise in areas rarely encountered by their colleagues in other departments, they are frequently consulted on specific aspects of commercial transactions. For example, at Nabarros we have found that the people best able to handle the complex drafting of company share incentive schemes are our trust lawyers, who have used their tax planning skills to produce some very interesting variations on the standard arrangements.

The lawyers

Now, the sort of people who handle private client work.

Anyone hoping to escape the pressures of mainstream commercial work will be disappointed. Individuals regard their personal affairs as having an urgency and importance which cannot be rationalized or explained away. Obviously, some matters really will not wait; instructions for a deathbed will cannot be deferred until tomorrow! In addition, private client work has its own particular stresses. Could you cope with a client who attends every meeting with his wife but then telephones you to make sure that his mistress (or mistresses) will be adequately provided for? Or one who has just had a terminal illness diagnosed? Family disputes have an acrimony rarely found in commercial litigation. There is also the phenomenon of 'OPM': other people's money. Experienced business clients who daily make judgement calls on multi-million pound deals for their company can become paralysed when asked to make a decision on committing their own personal wealth to a particular course of action.

The qualities necessary for a good private client lawyer? Really, all those one finds in any good solicitor, only more so! A good listener, sympathetic but detached. The ability to extract the important facts from a morass of irrelevancies. The creativity to design a sensible solution to the client's problem, and the confidence to convince the client to adopt it. A modicum of firmness, and an abundance of discretion.

So, if you think that the work of the commercial department of a large firm may not satisfy all your expectations of being a solicitor, why not consider a career in the 'other department', as a private client lawyer?

'We're looking for a partner with an eccentric name.'

A legal career in commerce, finance and industry

KAMLESH BAHL

Kamlesh Bahl is the Company Secretary and Manager, Legal Services for Data Logic Limited, an international software services company in the computer industry. She has recently been elected to the Law Society's Council and appointed a non-executive member of Parkside Health Authority. She is also a member of the Law Society's Race Relations Committee and was Chairman of the Law Society's Commerce and Industry Group 1988/89, which represents all solicitors employed in commerce, finance and industry.

The concept of solicitors working in commerce, finance and industry is relatively recent in the UK. Twenty-five years ago a solicitor going into industry was regarded as 'a loss to the profession'. Equally, solicitors in industry were seen as a necessary evil and the businessman would only go to his in-house solicitor when it was absolutely necessary, eg when the company was sued.

Today, the image of a solicitor in industry has dramatically changed. In almost every major commercial concern there are now in-house solicitors and the demand is rapidly increasing. In fact, comparisons are now drawn between UK in-house solicitors and the 'Corporate Counsel' in the USA who have a long and well-established tradition. So what are the advantages of being an in-house solicitor?

Firstly, the in-house solicitor is required to build up a thorough and detailed understanding of the business, the personalities in it and the way industry works in general. He or she must become familiar with the policies and strategies of the company and its particular sensitivities. He or she is then uniquely placed to give legal advice which is *relevant* to that organization and to make positive recommendations which the business can implement.

Secondly, the solicitor is available, not only when an emergency arises but at other times, too. The solicitor can play a preventative role, which means that the company seeks and gets legal advice earlier and puts this into effect when formulating its long and short-term strategies and policies.

Thirdly, the in-house solicitor plays a major role in multidisciplinary teams with people of different backgrounds and skills within the company where all are trying to achieve a common objective, eg a company acquisition, a joint venture agreement.

Fourthly and increasingly, the in-house solicitor is playing a critical role as a member of the company's management team. Most companies now recognize that the logical objective and factual approach that a legal training provides are critical skills required for management.

Fifthly, the complexity of legislation, and the increasing and detailed impact it now has on every aspect of an organization's operation, means readily available legal advice is now essential.

A recent survey showed that external solicitors are approximately three-and-a-half times more expensive to employ than in-house solicitors. An in-house legal department also provides better control over legal costs where external lawyers need to be used.

Also, more and more organizations, particularly with the advent of 1992, are becoming international in their outlook. The in-house solicitor has to be able to adapt to these changes and understand different cultures and negotiating styles and, depending on the employer's business, will often get involved in overseas negotiations.

So, what benefits are there for the in-house solicitor?

- He or she gets to know and understand the business fully and becomes commercially aware. This leads to the satisfaction of giving legal advice that is clear, practical and easy to understand and tailored to that organization's business needs.

- He or she gets involved from the beginning to the end in projects, for example in every aspect of the setting up of a subsidiary company in another country. He or she would consider, with a local lawyer, the relevant laws, the establishment of the company, and the legislation concerning the business operating in that country such as employment law, pensions, leasing of premises.

- He or she will get to meet and work closely with members of other professions and disciplines, and will have to work positively and constructively to find a solution for the company which addresses concerns from all members of the team.

A legal career in commerce, finance and industry 121

- The nature of the job means that there is always variety and the solicitor now has to have a wide knowledge of major developments, certainly in UK and EEC law.
- The in-house solicitor has the satisfaction of knowing that a contribution in the early stages of the company's policy formulations means that the company is acting legally and as a good corporate citizen.

The solicitor in commerce and industry is expected to be a person with good legal knowledge, who has a flexible and confident attitude and who can communicate clearly and simply. They are expected to be able to adapt, understand and help achieve a company's objectives both short and long-term. The solicitor has to be an individual who can work under pressure, to cope with unexpected and varied demands and to communicate with all levels of management within an organization. Usually the in-house solicitor operates as a general practitioner, ie to spot issues and advise generally on all areas of a company's business. However, many in-house solicitors also develop specialisms such as employment law, intellectual property law, and competition law which are relevant to the employer's business.

In-house solicitors and solicitors in private practice both have the same legal status and standing. The major difference is that generally in-house solicitors are employed to give advice on a full-time basis to one client, their employer. A solicitor in private practice will be retained, however, to deal with specific legal questions for a variety of clients. In practice, the in-house solicitor also has a number of clients, for example the various departments in a company such as financial, personnel, marketing and the directors of the company. In larger companies, the in-house solicitor often acts for the company's subsidiaries including overseas subsidiaries.

The avenues for career progression as a lawyer in commerce, finance and industry are also developing rapidly. There is, of course, the traditional aspiration of becoming the head of the legal department, which can now range from small to very large indeed. Another well-established career path is to become the company secretary and this usually means a place on the board. In recent years the particular contribution of in-house solicitors has been reorganized and there is now plenty of scope to develop in other management areas, eg finance, administration, marketing. There are now examples of solicitors who have achieved very high positions of responsibility in commerce, finance and industry, eg the company secretary at British Gas, and the current chairman of ICI. There are ample opportunities to develop in many different directions and into a variety of business areas to suit any particular talent or interest.

The major changes in industry in the UK, the need for greater efficiency and profitability, and the need to be international in outlook, have led to major changes in the demands made of the in-house solicitor. These changes, together with the developments in the role and perception of the in-house solicitor, mean that this is a highly demanding, challenging, exciting and now critical role.

Further information about a career as a solicitor in commerce and industry can be obtained from: Juliet Heasman, Committee Secretary, The Law Society's Commerce and Industry Group, The Law Society, 113 Chancery Lane, London WC2A 1PL. Tel: 071-242 1222.

The Government Legal Service

The Government Legal Service comprises almost 1,000 lawyers, who are employed in most departments of State and provide a comprehensive range of legal work for the government. A service of this size has certain clear advantages: for example, a proper career structure and training are available to all, and the possibility of moving between departments or between areas of work means that a government lawyer can either specialize or acquire wider experience.

It is impossible here to touch on more than a few of the activities of the Government Legal Service. There are few areas of the law in which the government does not have a crucial interest, and its lawyers are closely involved in the legislative process. They instruct Parliamentary Counsel on the drafting of primary legislation, themselves draft secondary legislation, and follow bills through Parliament, advising ministers and policy administrators at each stage as necessary. Other GLS posts offer a different perspective of more familiar types of work, such as conveyancing or employment law. The government is one of the largest employers and landowners in the country, and nearly all the consequent legal work is done in-house. The work of some government lawyers, for example in the areas of consumer protection or health and safety, brings a heightened sense of public service. There is plenty of scope for high quality advocacy. The GLS offers lawyers the chance to develop their skills in a unique legal environment at the centre of affairs of national or international importance.

Most government lawyers join after qualification, and all posts are open to both solicitors and barristers. There are no upper or lower age limits. Salary is regularly reviewed and offers opportunities for performance-related increments above the normal scale maximum. An attractive non-contributory pension scheme, generous paid leave allowance and a regular working week are further benefits. The career of every government lawyer is planned and developed with the assistance of a central, non-departmental management team who try to ensure that the GLS and its lawyers get the best out of each other.

Further details of the work of the GLS can be found by obtaining the brochure *Lawyers in Government*, free on application to the Lawyers'

Management Unit, Queen Anne's Chambers, 28 Broadway, London SW1H 9JS. In addition, there are a limited number of positions available in the GLS for trainee solicitors and barrister pupils. Further information can be obtained from the Lawyers' Management Unit at the above address.

The Crown Prosecution Service

BARRY HANCOCK

Barry Hancock qualified as a lawyer in 1978 having been articled in private practice and began his prosecuting career with the Sussex Police Authority. When the CPS began operating in 1986 he was appointed Branch Crown Prosecutor for West Sussex and later as a senior casework lawyer at CPS Headquarters. Barry took up his present position as Head of Recruitment in the summer of 1990.

General background

The Crown Prosecution Service (CPS) was launched in October 1986 and has already had a great impact on the criminal justice system. This is not surprising, since it is responsible for the conduct of all the criminal proceedings instituted by the police throughout England and Wales (with the exception of the most minor traffic offences).

Before 1986, the system had tended to work on a solicitor and client basis, with the police as the client. The Prosecution of Offences Act 1985 removed that relationship and established the independence of the CPS. It provided for the appointment of qualified barristers and solicitors as Crown Prosecutors, who are required to review the matter referred to them and decide whether or not a case should be prosecuted. Thus, once the police have completed their investigations and laid charges, CPS staff have to decide whether the case should proceed, to conduct the prosecution in the magistrates' court, and to brief counsel if the case goes on to the crown court.

The structure of the CPS

The Director of Public Prosecutions is head of the CPS and is situated at the Service's headquarters in London.

The CPS employs over 1,600 lawyers (more than any other organization) and 3,500 law clerks and support staff. There are over 100 offices grouped into thirty-one areas throughout England and Wales. The CPS has a Chief Executive and Deputy Director and each one of the thirty-one areas has a

Chief Crown Prosecutor. The DPP on behalf of the Service is answerable to the Attorney General who is the government minister responsible for the CPS.

Career opportunities

Both barristers and solicitors can work as lawyers in the CPS. Lawyers with limited or even no previous experience join in the grade of Crown Prosecutor. They receive training in the work of the CPS and spend much of their time prosecuting whole lists of cases in magistrates' courts. In this way they rapidly gain extensive experience of advocacy and criminal litigation. They also review cases, under the guidance of their more senior colleagues, to decide which should proceed, and they advise police officers on the merits of particular cases.

After two years satisfactory service there is the opportunity to be re-graded to Senior Crown Prosecutor. Lawyers with three or four years' relevant experience can be appointed directly as a Senior Crown Prosecutor. Further opportunities exist for particularly able lawyers to advance to the grade of Principal Crown Prosecutor. Principle Crown Prosecutors still regularly go to court but tend to concentrate on the more difficult and complex cases. They also guide and supervise their prosecutors and prepare them for wider responsibilities.

It is possible for lawyers to specialize in particular fields, such as juvenile work, or fraud cases. They can also seek promotion to Branch Crown Prosecutor. Branch Crown Prosecutors are lawyers responsible for a complete office or small group of offices. They still go to court, but are primarily managers of both the lawyers and the support staff in the office, who will include law clerks in a crown court section responsible for briefing counsel. Branch Crown Prosecutors report to the Chief Crown Prosecutor for the area.

Lawyers in the Service can remain in one office throughout their career. Often, however, they can increase their prospects of promotion, and gain wider experience, by moving between offices. Financial assistance is provided if this means moving house.

The Crown Prosecution Service therefore offers all lawyers the opportunity both to gain experience in all aspects of prosecution work and to rise to the most senior positions in the civil service.

Sponsored pupils and trainee solicitors in CPS

The CPS has two hundred places for both barristers who wish to undertake pupillage and for trainee solicitors wishing to become solicitors, where great emphasis is placed on ensuring that a thorough training is given.

The lawyer in local government

CHRISTOPHER ROBINSON

Christopher Robinson graduated from Cambridge in 1959 and until recently was County Secretary and Solicitor of Surrey. He is the Careers Promotion and Graduate Recruitment Coordinator for County Council Legal Departments in England and Wales.

Some personal views

'Why do you work in local government rather than private practice?' is the question most frequently put to you at university and polytechnic careers events around the country. Why indeed! A very fair and understandable question but not one that is easy to answer. On the other hand, our private practice colleagues find the reverse question even more difficult as they know much less about local government than we do about private practice.

Perhaps the first thing to stress is that we solicitors are all in one single profession with a common legal training. It is the similarities between our work rather than the differences which stand out. Even during articles it is only the working environment that is different. Movement between private sector and local government is becoming increasingly common early on in the professional career to the actual benefit of both sectors.

For those who wish to make the move into the private sector, the quality of local government professionals make them a much sought after and valued commodity – indeed, but for the training and experience we provide, the planning departments of many a City practice would have less partners! We in local government for our part appreciate the sometimes different approach that is brought to bear on our organizations and problems by those of our private practice colleagues who join us.

The main difference is, of course, that we have but one client, our council, with no need or indeed right to seek other clients elsewhere. In this respect we do, of course, have much in common with our commerce and industry group colleagues. In both these sectors the importance of the 'in-house lawyer' with an understanding of the client's organization and the background to problems that arise is recognized. The ability to participate in the formulation of policies and the working out of decisions means that many a potential legal difficulty, if not disaster, is averted at the outset, an opportunity much less frequently open to our private practice colleagues.

Even in the sixties, the acceptance of articles in local government rather than in private practice was considered rather strange. However, at that time the path to the most senior local authority administrative posts was almost invariably through the solicitor's qualification. That is no longer the case, but it is still possible for the solicitor with wider ambitions to progress into general management posts with the ultimate goal of becoming a chief executive, and many still do. However, it is also now easier to progress in your career as a specialist in a particular field.

Recruitment these days is not easy for anyone, but we are still able to attract good quality trainee solicitors and are beginning to find it easier to appoint assistant solicitors from amongst those who have served articles in private practice and have found the approach of City commercial practice not to their liking. However, local government still has some work to do to get its message across more widely to prospective recruits and so it is to some of my younger colleagues that I now turn to help me explain why they work for local government.

Allan graduated from Manchester University in 1981 and served his articles with Leicestershire County Council to which he was recruited under the SOCS Joint Recruitment Exercise before joining his present authority as an assistant in the child care team. He has since spent a spell as an assistant solicitor in their highways team and has recently been promoted to principal solicitor within a strengthened child care team. 'As a local government trainee solicitor I frequently had the opportunity of representing the authority in court. From day one as a solicitor, I thus had advocacy experience and have since enjoyed the diversity of forums in which a local authority advocate appears'.

Sarah graduated from Southampton University in 1980 and obtained the Law Society's Diploma in Local Government Law and Practice in 1987. She was with a district council immediately before her appointment in January 1988 as a senior solicitor in the education team of the legal department of a large county council. Within three months she had won promotion to head of that team. 'In recent years we have been faced with a steady stream of new legislation which we have had to master. I am currently working with my colleagues in the education department on problems in connection with the implementation of the government's major Education Reform Act. As in-house solicitors we are involved at the early stage of planning projects and are able to see their progress through the political decision-making process to completion. Often these are issues of considerable sensitivity and importance to the local community'.

Serena joined the same authority in September 1989 after serving articles in a medium-sized commercial practice in Central London. She graduated from Birmingham University in July 1986. She is working with Sarah in the education and social services team, which is facing a growing workload resulting from government policies for changes in school management and for care in the community. 'I joined specifically to practise in education and social services law, which I would not have had the chance to do had I stayed in private practice. I find the workload both interesting and stimulating, especially as I am involved as the new education legislation is beginning to take effect, with all its resultant problems. Many people tried to convince me not to leave private practice, as they perceived local government as being in some ways a 'second-class option'. However, I feel that people should give due consideration to a career in local government. On first impressions, it has certainly lived up to my expectations.'

Jane joined Surrey County Council as a trainee solicitor in 1988, after graduating from Trent Polytechnic and successfully passing her Law Society Final Examinations. She too was recruited through the SOCS Joint Recruitment Exercise and has recently completed her articles. She has stayed on with the authority as an assistant in their planning team. 'Life as a trainee solicitor in local government is both challenging and rewarding. With the aid of a structured training programme, I have gained a valuable insight into many new and exciting areas of law including planning, education and contract. I can certainly recommend such a career to anyone.'

Fiona graduated from King's College London in French. She served her articles in a large City practice and stayed on with them for three years in their commercial litigation department before joining her present county council. 'I enjoy the fact that I am no longer solely motivated by profit. As a commercial lawyer I was office bound dealing with a particular type of client and writing lots of letters. Now as a child care advocate I am out and about the country and working with people all the time, not only the people in difficulty but with other professionals. I particularly enjoy not having to hand over a case to a barrister at what is sometimes the most crucial point'.

Andrea having graduated at Trent Polytechnic in 1981 with a degree in social sciences spent a year abroad and time working with problem teenagers, and then in a law centre before taking her CPE at Wolverhampton

Polytechnic. She then joined a county council as a trainee solicitor and has recently attended the College of Law at Guildford for her LSFE Course, at their expense and on full salary. 'What surprised me about local government was the quality and quantity of commercial property work undertaken. As a local government officer I have also had rights of audience in the magistrates court whilst still a trainee solicitor. This has given me useful experience which is not available to my contemporaries in private practice'.

The options

Such then are the reasons why some colleagues joined and remain in local government, but what are the options for anyone considering a similar career? There are 449 separate and independant local authorities in England and Wales, which together a small number of statutory joint bodies are responsible for the provision to their communities of a range of important services. The principal services are:

> housing, education, social services, countryside amenities, recreation, libraries, museums, arts, police, fire-rescue, consumer protection, environmental health, highways and traffic, public transport, waste collection and disposal, planning and economic development.

In the seven metropolitan areas of Greater London, West Midlands, Greater Manchester, Merseyside, South Yorkshire, West Yorkshire and Tyne & Wear, a single tier of local authorities, the thirty-three London borough councils and the thirty-five Metropolitan district councils, together with some joint bodies of those councils, are responsible for all these services. In the rest of the country there is a two-tier structure of forty-seven county councils and 333 Shire district councils supported in most areas by parish, town or community councils. The services are provided in most cases by either county or district council but in respect of some services responsibility is split or shared.

Most, but not all, local authorities have an 'in-house' legal service. However, by no means all recruit trainee solicitors. Of those that do, few recruit more than one a year and many only one every other year. In all, local authorities seek to appoint about 150 trainees for each year, some two years ahead of appointment, others one year ahead, but the majority only shortly before appointment. Vacancies will usually be notified direct to Careers Advisory Services and/or advertised in the *Law Society Gazette* and the spring and autumn special student editions of the *Lawyer*.

The size of legal departments and the range of work undertaken varies considerably but it is principally dictated by the following factors:

- The functions for which the authority is responsible;
- The size of the population it serves; and
- The degree to which work is as a matter of policy contracted out to the private sector.

Broadly speaking county councils, London borough councils and Metropolitan councils have the broadest range of functions, serve the largest populations and will, therefore, have the larger legal departments. However, there are also some Shire district councils serving large populations with, in consequence, large legal departments, and all local authorities recruiting trainee solicitors can offer the range and quality of experience necessary to satisfy not merely Law Society requirements but also the intellectual demands and interest of the most demanding individual.

The local government lawyer

Making the choice – some questions answered

Do local authorities sponsor students?

Bursary schemes are being developed by some and others participate in the METRA Sponsorship Scheme. Ask for more details.

How can I find out more about life in a local authority legal department?

If, having seen our video, read our brochures and studied profiles, you would like to see for yourself you can always take vacation work experience or visit a legal department. Ask for more details.

Where will I be able to work?

Almost anywhere in England and Wales if vacancies currently exist for trainee solicitors. Equally you will be able to move to another area on admission or later in your career. Ask for our vacancy lists.

Would I be the only trainee solicitor?

Probably yes, except in some of the larger authorities that take one or more each year. However, it is unlikely that you will be the only graduate trainee starting work in the authority at the time, as other local authority professions have similar training arrangements.

Do local authorities accept mature students as trainee solicitors?

Very definitely 'yes'. Appointments are made on merit regardless of age, race or gender. Disabled applicants are encouraged to apply.

Will I be able to specialize after admission?

Yes, if you wish to do so and certainly later in your career. But a wider range of experience is desirable in the first few years after admission.

Would private practice experience count against me if I applied later in my career for a local authority post?

On the contrary such experience is increasingly regarded as an asset. There is now far more 'cross fertilization' between the public and private sector.

Would local authority training prevent a later career move into the private sector?

No, but we would like to think that you would not wish to do so having once worked for a local authority. Some local authority experience, particularly in planning and court work, is much sought after in the private sector.

Do local authorities have career break arrangements?

Local authorities generally operate flexible working hours and employ staff on a part-time or job share basis and therefore provide a sympathetic working environment for those with family commitments. Even part-time working as a trainee solicitor is now possible.

What about training after admission?

Local authorities have a good record in encouraging and paying for continuing professional and management training for their staff. The Law Society Local Government Group have appointed a Director of Training to ensure the provision of an adequate range of relevant courses, seminars and workshops.

Would there be any scope for progression into general management later in my career?

Local authority chief executives are no longer always lawyers but many still are and such posts will remain as open to senior managers in the local government legal service as they will to managers in other professional disciplines.

The choice is yours

In my personal view the career prospects for the able local government lawyer are better today than they ever have been. There is no shortage of challenging legal problems awaiting solution. The local government lawyer has a career which offers:

At all stages

• Personal responsibility but with guidance appropriate to experience and ability
• Challenging problems requiring practical solutions
• A political and corporate environment in a wide range of authorities
• The attraction of multi-disciplinary working
• Flexible working conditions particularly attractive to those wishing to return to work either full-time or part-time
• Genuine equal opportunities for all.

During training

• Broad range of work related to the services that the authority provides and satisfying Law Society requirements
• A competitive salary
• Opportunities for advocacy not available to colleagues in other sectors.

After admission

• Professional development through management training and continuing professional education – particularly for the Local Government Diploma, the Law Society's first specialist qualification
• A wide range of high quality work
• Opportunity to specialize
• Service to the local community including voluntary and business sectors
• Long-term prospects with scope for progressing into legal and general management
• Experience valued by private practice
• Openings for those trained and experienced in other sectors.

Further enquiries

If you would like to find out more about a legal career in local government, before making your decision:

(a) Ask your Careers Service Adviser for a copy of our careers brochure and of our profiles booklet.

(b) See also our ten minute video 'More than just a career' which the Careers Service will have in their Resource Centre.

(c) Visit the lawyers local government stand at the next Careers Fair.

(d) Ask your Careers Service Adviser to put you in touch with one of our liaison officers.

(e) Get in touch with your local council's solicitor who will be pleased to talk to you and may be able to offer work experience.

(f) Write to me as Careers Promotion and Recruitment Coordinator, The Coach House, Station Road, Godalming, Surrey GU7 1EX.

The Magistrates' Courts Service

STEPHEN CAVEN

Stephen Caven graduated in law in 1978. Having obtained articles with a medium sized legal practice in Greater Manchester he remained with the firm after qualifying, eventually managing a branch office. In 1986, he 'stepped off the conveyancing treadmill' and embarked on a career as a court clerk in the Magistrates' Courts Service. He is now Principal Assistant at Oldham Magistrates' Court with responsibility for a team of ten court clerks.

General background

Magistrates have played an important role in the administration of justice for more than six centuries. There are currently some 28,000 lay magistrates recruited from all walks of life. They are advised on matters of law and legal procedure by court clerks. There are currently over 2,000 court clerks. A large proportion of court clerks are professionally qualified as either solicitors or barristers.

Because magistrates have been part of the fabric of the legal system for so long, much of the associated terminology and nomenclature has an archaic or anachronistic flavour. For example, magistrates are also known as justices of the peace. They are appointed to one of the fifty-eight commission areas (outside London these are essentially counties). Within a commission area they are assigned to a bench which covers one of the 500 or so Petty Sessional Divisions (which are the catchment areas for court business). Their legal advisers are known as clerks, despite the fact that many of them are solicitors or barristers of many years' standing.

This outdated appearance is, however, deceptive. Magistrates, advised by their clerks, are called upon to make judicial decisions involving a staggering variety of contemporary issues, reflecting the increasingly complex nature of modern society. Matters within their jurisdiction range from determining whether a child should be taken from its parents and placed in the care of the local authority because of alleged abuse, to deciding whether a new casino should be licensed.

The work of the courts

Every person charged with a criminal offence, however serious or sophisticated, must appear initially before a magistrates' court. The vast majority (around ninety-five per cent) of all criminal prosecutions are concluded there. Justices are empowered to determine finally, in appropriate cases, allegations such as burglary or the possession of controlled drugs. They also deal with matters which can only proceed at summary level including driving with excess alcohol or speeding. As regards the most serious offences such as murder or rape, magistrates will decide whether the accused is to be granted bail, and they may be required to decide in committal proceedings, if sufficient evidence has been adduced to justify the continuation of the trial before a jury at the Crown Court.

It is a common misconception that magistrates' courts are solely concerned with criminal proceedings. In fact magistrates have a wide ranging civil jurisdiction. They have the primary responsibility for the licensing of premises where alcohol is sold, from the corner off-licence to the most exclusive restaurant. Their jurisdiction also encompasses the licensing of betting and gaming.

Justices have always had a central role in proceedings relating to children. Following the implementation of the Children Act 1989 this role has been further expanded. In the area of private law, dealing with the resolution of disputes between individuals over the upbringing of children, magistrates have been given, in many cases, concurrent jurisdiction with the higher courts.

Proceedings in the field of public law, concerned with the intervention of the state to protect children at risk, are almost invariably commenced in magistrates' courts. A great deal of understanding and expertise on the part of justices and their legal advisers is required in responding to the sensitive issues raised by such proceedings.

A career as a court clerk

Magistrates are essentially lay persons who serve on their local bench on a voluntary basis. In an era of increasingly complex legislation they rely to a great extent on their legal adviser, the court clerk, for guidance on questions of law. Most courts have a team of court clerks grouped under the clerk to the justices, who has the overall responsibility for the smooth running of the court.

There is a growing emphasis on managing resources efficiently and making the best use of technological advances in the courts' service. Effective management and administration are essential. But the primary duty of the clerk to the justices has always been to provide legal advice to justices. On a day-to-day basis this function will be discharged by court clerks who have the responsibility for all matters listed in a particular court.

A large number of court clerks are solicitors or barristers and in order to be appointed as a clerk to the justices it is necessary to be a solicitor or barrister of five years' standing. It is possible to become a court clerk by obtaining a Diploma in Magisterial Law, which requires attendance on a three-year part-time course whilst employed in the courts' service. However, most courts recognize the value of professionally qualified court clerks and actively seek to recruit recently qualified solicitors or barristers. For those working in the courts sponsorship is usually available to candidates for the Law Society or Bar Finals. Articles of clerkship are normally available although court clerks with five years' experience are exempt from the requirement to serve articles before admission.

The diverse nature of proceedings in magistrates' courts means that the work of a court clerk is usually stimulating and interesting. There are opportunities to develop expertise in a wide variety of legal fields. In addition, clerks with the ability to explain legal principles in a clear and concise manner are in great demand for the continuing programme of magistrates' training. The large number of courts in England and Wales provide a wide range of alternative options, both in terms of geographical area and the size of court. Whether it be in a busy urban environment or a small rural courthouse, the Magistrates' Courts Service offers the possibility of a challenging and rewarding career.

Working at a law centre

MELODY PAVEY

Melody Pavey is a Policy and Research Officer at the Law Centres Federation, having previously worked in a South London law centre. Her nine years' experience enables her to give a valuable insight into this important part of our legal structure.

In the UK, sixty law centres (LCs) advise and represent people and groups within their locality. Most law centres receive a grant from their local authorities for salaries and running costs. A very few are financed from central government via the Lord Chancellor's Legal Aid Board. They are run by management committees, made up of consumers and community representatives, who also decide on the general direction of the law centre. In this way, law centres aim to tailor their service to the needs of the community.

The role

The remit of a law centre is to provide legal support to those with most need. The order of priorities within this broad aim is usually fine tuned by the management committee, but the areas which always figure are housing in the rented sector, employment in relation to the rights of the employee at work, immigration and nationality; welfare rights and benefits; children's rights in respect of education, care and wardship and in a few cases, crime. Given their role and the need to target their limited resources, LCs do not handle adult crime, conveyancing, probate, divorce or commercial work, as these are covered by the private sector.

Careers in a law centre

To be allowed to operate, a LC has to employ at least one solicitor of three or more years' post-qualification experience. Barristers can also be employed and indeed this is the only salaried work permitted to a practising member of the Bar. A LC needs to incorporate a wide range of skills, including representing clients in court, in front of tribunals and in negotiations with other bodies. In addition to their legally qualified staff, most centres employ specialist advice and community workers, as many problems have more than just a legal dimension.

Working in this environment you will need to talk to clients sympathetically encouraging and assisting them to deal with as much of their problems themselves. You work with community groups, giving talks and writing leaflets that demystify the law and make it accessible to all members of the community.

LCs are able, so long as they satisfy the Law Society rules, to take on trainee solicitors. This is still a relatively rare occurrence, if only because resources are stretched and no systematic scheme exists at present.

The Law Centres Federation

The umbrella body representing all LCs is the Law Centres Federation, which helps in the development of the services and structure of existing LCs and in the expansion of the national network. In addition, it publicizes the work of the LCs, acts as a conduit to government based on experience gained by its members, so influencing both existing policy and forthcoming legislation, and continues the ceaseless campaign for secure funding.

Further information, and in particular the third edition of the well-known publication *The Case for Law Centres*, is available by writing to The Law Centres Federation, Duchess House, 18-19 Warren Street, London W1P 5DB. Tel:071-387 8570.

Transferring from the Law Society to the Bar

Every year, just as a number of barristers decide that they would prefer, for a whole range of reasons, to become solicitors, so every year a similar impulse causes a number of solicitors to apply to transfer to the Bar. 'Qualified legal practitioners', with experience, usually receive a favourable hearing as the Bar Council values the experience they bring.

In practical terms, at present, the procedure for transfer is as follows (though the European Directive to allow in EC lawyers might result in some changes in the near future): The solicitor is asked by the Joint Regulations Committee to obtain two certificates of good character, one usually from the employer/senior partner and one from a member of the Council of the Law Society or someone of similar standing. A certificate of qualification as a solicitor is also required, as is evidence that the applicant intends to take up practice at the Bar. The applicant is asked to join an Inn and complete four dining terms before being called to the Bar. No admission is possible before the solicitor's name has been removed from the Law Society's Roll.

A former solicitor is not usually required to pass any of the examinations in the core subjects, or any section of the Bar Examination except Sections III (civil and criminal procedure) and IV (evidence). The Joint Regulations Committee has discretion to grant exemption from these and from the practical exercises and this discretion is exercised where sufficient experience and expertise is apparent in the candidate. Pupillage may be deemed inappropriate but this exemption is again dependent on individual cases and may in future depend to a greater extent on advocacy experience.

Given the existence of two branches to the legal profession, it is desirable for a mechanism to exist that allows lawyers to redirect their career. Both branches benefit and this flexibility ensures that valuable practitioners, who might otherwise leave, remain in the profession.

Copies of the full regulations in this area can be obtained from the Inn's of Court School of Law, 4 Gray's Inn Place, London WC1R 5DX (Tel: 071-404 5787).

Information and statistics

Introduction

The information and statistics set out in this chapter and the one in Part III are extracts from the Annual Statistical Report of the Law Society. The report was compiled by Stephen Harwood of the Law Society's Research and Policy Planning Unit who has produced quite the most comprehensive analysis of the profession available to date. What follows here can only be a subjective selection and for a fuller and thus more accurate picture, it is recommended that a copy of the report is purchased at £14.50 from Chancery Lane.

Routes to admission to the Roll

There are nine routes to qualification as a solicitor, which are:

(a) Law graduate
(b) Non-law graduate
(c) School-leaver
(d) Mature student
(e) Overseas solicitor (transfer)
(f) Barrister (transfer)
(g) Scots/N. Irish solicitor (transfer)
(h) Fellow of the Institute of Legal Executives (FILEX)
(i) Justices' clerks

The shortest route to qualification is by law degree, where training can be completed in three years after obtaining a degree. The vast majority of entrants to the profession choose this route, with 2,508 (sixty-seven per cent) of those admitted in 1989-90 being law graduates. Non-law graduates have to undertake a conversion course, the Common Professional Examination (CPE), which can be completed in a year. They then proceed to qualify in the same way as a law graduate. This is the second most popular route to admission, with 549 (fifteen per cent) qualifying by this route in 1989-90, a figure which has varied little in the recent past. In 1989-90, therefore, some eighty-two per cent of newly admitted solicitors were graduates and the supply of graduates is therefore a crucial factor influencing the size of the profession at a time when the profession is seeking more and more recruits. School-leavers and mature students (over twenty-five with no degree) can still enter the profession. The former must pass the Solicitors First Examination in addition to the Final Examination and undertake five-year articles, or four-year articles with one year on a course for the Finals. Mature students must pass the CPE and Final Examination and complete two-year articles. The number qualifying by these routes is tiny with just one school leaver and one mature student being admitted in 1989.

The other routes to admission are by transfer from another sector of the legal profession to the solicitors' profession. Small numbers of barristers and overseas solicitors are admitted to the profession each year though this number is rising. Barristers represented just over four per cent of admissions in 1989-90, whilst overseas solicitors were ten per cent of admissions in 1989-90. A detailed breakdown of those admitted in 1989-90 is presented below.

Route to admission of solicitors admitted to the Roll in the years to 31st July 1989 and 1990

Route	Number admitted to 31st July 1989	%	Number admitted to 31st July 1990	%
Law graduate	2,518	73.3	2,508	67.3
Non-law graduate	476	13.9	549	14.7
School-leaver	10	0.3	1	0.0
Mature student	3	0.1	1	0.0
Overseas solicitor	241	7.0	388	10.4
Barrister	94	2.7	129	3.5
Scot/N. Ireland solicitor	18	0.5	63	1.7
FILEX (Legal executives)	54	1.6	53	1.4
Justices' clerks	20	0.6	37	1.0
Total	3,434	100.0	3,729	100.0

Graduates

Of all solicitors admitted in the year 1st August 1989 to 31st July 1990, eighty-two per cent were graduates. Of these sixty-seven per cent were law graduates. As such, they represent the most important source of recruits to the solicitors' profession.

The table below shows the numbers of university and polytechnic graduates for each of the last five years.

Numbers of law graduates 1985-1989

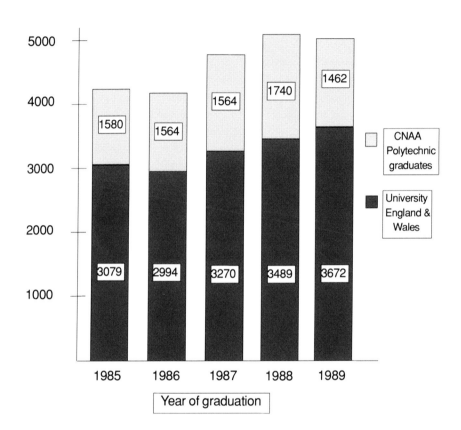

Solicitors Final Examination

The Law Society's Final Examination is a course which, with very few exceptions, must be undertaken for qualification as a solicitor. The course lasts for one academic year. The table overleaf shows the number of places provided for the academic years 1988/89, 1989/90 and 1990-91. The increase in the number of places being offered for 1989/90 was largely attributable to the opening of the new branch of the College of Law in York, in response to the increasing demand for solicitors.

**Places on the Solicitors Final Examination course 1988/89, 1989/90 &
1990/91**

	1988/89	1989/90	1990-91
The College of Law – London, Chancery Lane	336	336	425
London, Lancaster Gate	390	430	550
Guildford	900	954	1,000
Chester	900	1,010	1,218
York	500	770	
Birmingham Polytechnic	57	130	120
Bristol Polytechnic	174	160	200
Leeds Polytechnic	102	100	100
Leicester Polytechnic	–	–	80
City of London Polytechnic	142	100	100
Manchester Polytechnic	115	150	175
Newcastle-upon-Tyne Polytechnic	93	100	110
Trent Polytechnic (Nottingham)	130	125	125
Wolverhampton Polytechnic	41	75	75
Total places	3,380	4,170	5,048

Statistics on the results of the Final Examinations have in the past been
published in the Law Society's Gazette. The table below provides a summary
of these statistics. Not only are the number of women attempting the solicitors
finals on the increase, but women are continually achieving a much higher
pass rate than men.

**Results of first time candidates attempting the summer Solicitors Final
Examinations 1985–89**

	Candidates sitting the Final Examination			Numbers (and percentages) passing the Final Examination		
Year	Men	Women	Total	Men	Women	Total
1985	1,757	1,479	3,236	961 (54.6%)	908 (61.4%)	1,869 (57.8%)
1986	1,667	1,575	3,242	902 (54.1%)	1,046 (66.4%)	1,948 (60.1%)
1987	1,615	1,620	3,235	959 (59.4%)	1,100 (67.9%)	2,059 (63.6%)
1988	1,654	1,662	3,316	1,145 (69.2%)	1,234 (74.2%)	2,379 (71.7%)
1989	–	–	3,511	–	–	2,558 (72.9%)

Articles registered

As part of a solicitor's training, a trainee solicitor is required to work in a solicitor's office in order to gain experience in the work undertaken by solicitors. These periods of training are called 'articles' and the student is described as being 'articled' to a particular solicitor, the 'principal', who is responsible for his or her training.

The majority of trainee solicitors are required to complete two-year articles, although a tiny minority seeking entry to the profession direct from school may serve up to five years' articles. A deed of articles is drawn up between solicitor and clerk and this has to be registered with the Law Society.

There were 3,254 new articles entered into in the year 1st August 1989 to 31st July 1990 (this excludes articles which have been transferred or extended). Of these, fifty-two per cent were registered by women – the same number as last year. This next table shows a breakdown of articles entered into by men and women by region. The regions are a combination of local law societies which correspond most closely to Government Standard Regions. Unfortunately, student records failed to record the location of articles in forty cases.

New articles entered into between 1st Aug and 31st July 1988/89 and 1989/90

	New articles 1988/89			New articles 1989/90		
Region	*Men*	*Women*	*Total*	*Men*	*Women*	*Total*
North	239	229	468	278	295	573
Midlands	144	192	336	166	178	344
Wales	65	52	117	64	69	133
South West	79	92	171	85	87	172
South East	153	226	379	165	231	396
Outer London	119	137	256	116	140	256
Inner London	655	647	1,302	680	688	1,369
All Regions	1,454	1,575	3,029	1,554	1,688	3,243
	(1,464)	(1,594)	(3,058)*	(1,559)	(1,695)	(3,254)*

* Figures in brackets are actual totals of articles entered into. Some student records do not identify region.

Not so long ago trainee solicitors had to pay for the privilege of being articled to a solicitor, but firms now employ trainee solicitors and are required to pay them at least the minimum salaries each year. The Law Society's

Council also fixes minimum rates which must apply across England and Wales. Past and current national minimum rates are set out below.

National minimum starting salaries for trainee solicitors

Effective date	*Inner London*	*Outer London*	*Elsewhere*
From 1/8/87	£6,600	£6,100	£5,200
From 1/8/88	£7,200	£6,900	£6,000
From 1/8/89	£8,500	£8,200	£7,300
From 1/8/90	£9,900	£9,600	£8,700
From 1/8/91	£11,300	£11,000	£10,100

The table below shows the average 1989-90 starting salaries of trainee solicitors entering articles. The percentage of clerks on the national minimum salary laid down by the Law Society is also shown. The percentages on the minimum salary have declined in all areas compared to previous years. In 1987/88 nineteen per cent of all new trainee solicitors were being paid the national minimum salary, in 1989/90 just 9.4 per cent were on the minimum.

Starting salaries of trainees solicitors 1989/90

Region	*Average salary*	*Percentage on minimum salary*	*Number of cases*
North	£8,510	27.1%	573
Midlands	£9,157	12.0%	344
Wales	£8,071	47.4%	133
South West	£9,135	5.8%	172
South East	£9,252	5.1%	396
Outer London	£11,215	3.9%	256
Inner London	£14,172	0.04%	1,369
All regions	£9,537	9.4%	3,243

Admissions to the Roll

The numbers of solicitors admitted to the Roll during the year up to 31st July 1990 was 3,729, an increase of 8.6 per cent on the previous year. This was the highest number of solicitors ever admitted in one year.

The table below provides a breakdown of the sex of solicitors admitted in recent years.

Numbers of solicitors admitted to the Roll

Year	Total	Men	%	Women	%
1985	2,683	1,572	58.6	1,111	41.4
1986	2,725	1,524	55.9	1,201	44.1
1987	2,973	1,626	54.7	1,347	45.3
1988	3,244	1,750	53.9	1,494	46.1
1988-89*	3,434	1,834	53.4	1,600	46.6
1989-90	3,729	1,990	53.4	1,739	46.6

* Date of recording changed to year 1st August to 31st July.

Part V
Becoming a barrister

What does a barrister do?

What makes a barrister different from a solicitor? What does he spend his time doing? The answer depends partly on his type of practice. It might be a purely criminal practice where he will both prosecute and defend people in the crown court and magistrates' courts, or it might be that he specializes in shipping law or patents or libel. However, broadly speaking, he or she may provide two things: an expert opinion, or powers of persuasion.

Unlike solicitors, the barrister has no direct contact with the public. He accepts his instructions to advise or act on a client's behalf through a solicitor. Recently, the Bar has changed its Code of Conduct to allow other professions to brief barristers on behalf of their clients in certain cases, but there is still no daily contact with the client in the way that the solicitor has. The reason for this lies not in any sense of exclusiveness, but in the different roles which each of these lawyers is designed to play.

The division of role, and often work, between the professions is much like that of GP and consultant. Solicitor and barrister are both lawyers, but each has different and complementary skills. The solicitor, like the GP, is the first point of contact for the public. He interviews his clients and finds out what their particular problem is. He collects all the evidence surrounding the matter which might be useful, taking notes and arranging for clarification of anything outstanding so that he can build up an accurate picture of the whole matter. If it can then be easily resolved, he will handle it himself. If it cannot be, or is otherwise complicated, he will want a second opinion from a specialist as to the likely consequences.

This is where the barrister comes in. He will often receive instructions in the form of 'counsel to advise', where he will refine the points in issue presented by the solicitor or other professional and map out the way the courts would currently be likely to decide them. At the next stage, he might be asked to draft the pleadings – to draw up the precise allegations of fact which are to be presented before the court, or to draft the other formal documents and affidavits which are necessary for court proceedings. Finally he will go into the court himself and present the case, for which he is particularly trained.

This means that, in practice, the barrister divides his time between advising on problems in writing and in conferences (ie meetings between barrister, solicitor/other professional and client), and taking the matter further by moulding it into a case, ready for presentation in court, and then appearing on his client's behalf to argue it.

Once in court, his particular skills as an advocate, which are developed by regular appearances and which depend on regular practice, come into play. Here he presents and analyses facts, adduces evidence by oral examination and cross-examination of witnesses, and argues law.

It is on this basis that barristers have to date been accorded the sole right of audience (ie the ability to present cases) in the higher courts in our legal system.

All these tasks mean that the barrister's professional life involves irregular and often long hours and also a great deal of time travelling and waiting around at court. Work will often come in concentrated doses. Instructions may be received minutes rather than days before a hearing.

So, what are the qualities that distinguish a barrister?

- He or she must have the intellectual qualities which any good lawyer needs.
- A barrister must have physical and mental stamina.
- A barrister must enjoy solving problems.
- A barrister must be able to communicate effectively with all sorts of people and enjoy doing so. He will be expected to deal with people from all walks of life, some articulate, some not, some intelligent, others less so.
- A barrister needs a highly enquiring mind, one that is curious about all things – cases have been won because the advocate happened to have some piece of general or specialist knowledge at the back of his mind which he was able to draw out at the crucial moment.
- He or she must be someone who can cope with the insecurity and uncertainty of being self-employed in a highly competitive profession.

The reward, when success comes, is a sense of personal achievement and self-fulfilment that is hard to match. The Bar is competitive – you pitch your skills daily against other men and women in the courts and live or die by your reputation as an advocate – but it is also highly supportive and friendly. And like other practising lawyers, you are constantly reminded that your work has a genuine and useful bearing on the lives of your clients.

Routes into the profession

SUSAN BLAKE

Susan Blake LLM, MA, was called to the Bar in 1976 and is now Reader in Law at the Council of Legal Education. She is the Course Director of the Vocational Course and played a substantial role in its development.

In this chapter reference will be made to the Council of Legal Education which operates as the governing body of the Inns of Court School of Law and is responsible for the conduct of the Bar Examination and for the Assessment process on the Vocational Course, and to the Inns of Court School of Law (ICSL) which provides the teaching for the Vocational Course but not for the Bar Examination. The address of both bodies is: 4 Grays Inn Place, London WC1R 5DX. Tel: 071-404 5787.

How can I judge if the Bar is for me?

Before choosing a career in law and/or deciding on which branch of the legal profession to join, it is advisable to spend time in a set of chambers. Many sets offer 'mini-pupillages'. These provide an ideal opportunity to experience first hand the full range of work which the Bar does and to soak up the atmosphere of the life style of the barrister. Time invested in a mini-pupillage will help you to know whether the Bar is for you – to know whether you have the determination to succeed in a profession where self-confidence is crucial and where the ability to manage yourself and your time very efficiently is an absolute necessity. If you need someone behind you to tell you what to do and when to do it – or if you are shy of hard work – the Bar is not for you. Barristers are self-motivated and self-starting – you must know yourself and whether you are the kind of person who can cope with this life style.

For information about how to obtain a mini-pupillage contact the General Council of the Bar or the student officer of any of the four Inns of Court.

Vocational training

The only route to qualification for those intending to enter pupillage, to obtain a practising certificate and to become a practising barrister in the territory of any member state of the European Community, is through the successful completion of the Vocational Course. This course is only available at the Inns of Court School of Law.

The Bar Examination is held for those who wish to be called to the Bar of England and Wales but who do not intend to practise as a barrister in any member state of the European Community and for those who, having sat the Bar Examination already, have yet to be successful in it. (Transitional arrangements will operate for a time to enable those who were partly qualified as at Michaelmas 1989 under the Bar Examination system to complete their training and then to practise as a barrister.)

Who is qualified for entry onto the Vocational Course at the Inns of Court School of Law (ICSL)?

Those who are members of one of the four Inns of Court *and* who have successfully completed the 'academic stage' of their training *and* intend to practise as a barrister in any member state of the European Community are entitled to enrol on the Vocational Course. It is important to realize that anyone who intends to practise as a barrister in any member state of the European Community, whether immediately or in the future, must successfully complete the Vocational Course at the ICSL.

The 'academic stage' of training can be completed in the following ways:

Law graduates

Law graduates can qualify for entry onto the Vocational Course or to take the Bar Examination (for the latter, see below) by successfully completing, at the required standard, a 'qualifying law degree' in law or in law combined with other subjects. In either case the degree must include the so-called 'core legal subjects' (namely: the law of contract, criminal law, constitutional and administrative law, land law, the law of torts and equity and trusts) and, in each of these six subjects, a satisfactory level of attainment must have been achieved.

A 'qualifying law degree'
In order for a degree to be a 'qualifying' one it must have been granted by an institution situated in England and Wales and be approved for this purpose by the Council of Legal Education, and normally have been obtained within the last five years (for the rules which apply when a degree is more than five years old see the Consolidated Regulations available in the Calendar from the Council of Legal Education). A list of approved degrees is available from the Council of Legal Education.

The required standard of degree
This is normally that of lower second class or better. In cases where there were very exceptional circumstances which adversely affected the applicant's performance on his or her degree programme and hence the quality of the degree obtained, graduates with a third class degree, or a pass or unclassified degree, may be considered for entry. Each case is considered on its merits and enquiry should be made of the Assistant to the Dean, Inns of Court School of Law.

The 'core legal subjects'
It is recognized that the content of law degrees varies from institution to institution; some include the six 'core legal subjects' as a compulsory part of their degree course whilst others may offer these subjects as options. A student who wishes to become a barrister must study these subjects and, in general, it is often easier to study them as part of the degree. Institutions may use different titles to describe these subjects and sometimes parts of these subjects are taught in combination with other subjects. In most of these cases the Council of Legal Education will have agreed with the institution concerned that it will treat these subjects as the equivalent of the core legal subject(s). A graduate whose degree does not include in some form or other all six 'core legal subjects', or who has failed one or more of these subjects (whilst nevertheless achieving a satisfactory standard of degree overall) can make up the deficit in the Common Professional Examination. Information about the Common Professional Examination can be obtained from the Council of Legal Education.

Non-law graduates
Non-law graduates can qualify for admission by successfully completing, at the required standard, a degree in a subject or subjects other than law studied at a

university, polytechnic or other institution in the United Kingdom or the Republic of Ireland, and successfully completing a one-year full time course leading to the Common Professional Examination.

The Common Professional Examination (CPE)
The course leading to the Common Professional Examination provides tuition in the 'core legal subjects' (detailed above) and gives sufficient grounding in the basic principles of law and legal method as necessary to enable non-law graduates to undertake the practical training on the Vocational Course. The CPE course is particularly intensive since students are required to study the 'core legal subjects' in the same depth as on a law degree course but over a very much shorter period of time than would traditionally be spent on these subjects on a law degree. Information about the CPE courses can be obtained from the Council of Legal Education.

The required standard of degree
Normally only those degrees which are obtained at a lower second class or better standard will entitle their holder to admission onto the Vocational Course, subject to the very exceptional circumstances explained above.

Will a non-law graduate suffer any disadvantage?
In a word, No! Many extremely successful members of the Bar and some of our most revered judges are graduates in disciplines other than law. In some specialist areas of practice being a graduate from another field is almost a prerequisite for success, for example at the Patent Bar many successful practitioners have science or engineering backgrounds. In any event, barristers often need to draw on their knowledge and understanding of business and commercial practices in order to find the most sensible solution to the lay client's particular problem – a broad educational or experiential background provides a foundation from which the practical solution can most easily be found.

Non-graduate mature students
These may qualify for admission if they have been accepted by an Inn of Court as having exceptional ability in an academic, professional, business or administrative field and have successfully completed a full-time two-year course offered at the Polytechnic of Central London. (Further information

can be obtained from the Eligibility Officer at the Inns of Court School of Law.)

The special course
This consists of the 'core legal subjects' (detailed above) and two other legal subjects which can be chosen from the list of subjects on offer. (Information about this course can be obtained from the Polytechnic of Central London.)

Graduates of overseas institutions
Graduates in law
These must first apply for a Certificate of Eligibility from the Council of Legal Education. This will specify the form of study and examination which must be undertaken in order to complete the academic stage of training. Generally, most graduates will be required to take some further examinations in the 'core legal subjects'.

Non-law graduates
Again these must first apply for a Certificate of Eligibility from the Council of Legal Education. This will specify the form of study and examination which must be undertaken in order to complete the academic stage of training. Such graduates must show a good knowledge of the English language and either show an intention to or have reasonable grounds to expect to practise at the Bar of England and Wales, or an intention to use the qualification in the course of a profession or employment in England and Wales, and have Home Office permission to remain in the UK to do so.

Those not intending to practise at the Bar of England and Wales

Those who do not intend to practise at the Bar of England and Wales and who are therefore usually not eligible to enrol on the Vocational Course but wish to be called to the Bar, must pass the Bar Examination. The syllabuses for the Bar Examination are published annually in the Calendar and for the time being the examination will continue in the same format. Any changes to the nature or format of this examination will be announced by the Council of Legal Education well in advance of the Trinity examination. Those who wish to qualify by this route must be members of one of the four Inns of Court and have successfully completed the 'academic stage of training' described fully above. The Inns of Court School of Law no longer offers a course to prepare candidates for this examination. However, courses are run by four institutions in the London area with whom the Council of Legal Education has made arrangements and the addresses of those institutions which offer such courses can be obtained from the Information Officer at the Council of Legal Education.

NB. Those from certain dependent territories may be entitled in limited circumstances to enrol on the Vocational Course provided that they can show an intention to practise in the legal profession of that territory.

Admission of qualified legal practitioners to the English Bar

Special provision is made to enable such persons to apply to the Joint Regulations Committee to be considered for exemption from the normal process for qualification to practise as a barrister. Consideration is given to the examinations which the applicant has passed and to his or her practical or other experience.

Pupillage

A person who intends to practise as a barrister is required to complete a twelve-month period in pupillage which is divided into the non-practising first six months and the practising second six months. It is for each individual to make their own arrangements for pupillage, but information is available as to pupillages offered. Information is best sought through student officers of any of the four Inns of Court. The ICSL can only give limited general advice on pupillage for those taking the Vocational Course.

The formal training – the Vocational Course and the Bar Examination

SUSAN BLAKE

Susan Blake LLM, MA, was called to the Bar in 1976 and is now Reader in Law at the Council of Legal Education. She is the Course Director of the Vocational Course and played a substantial role in its development.

There are two different arrangements governing the formal training to be called to the Bar of England and Wales. The choice of which training scheme to follow depends on an individual's future intentions as to the geographical location of his or her practice. Those who intend to practise as a barrister in a member state of the European Community must successfully complete the Vocational Course at the Inns of Court School of Law. Those who do not intend to practise as a barrister in a member state of the European Community but, who nevertheless wish to be called to the Bar of England and Wales, must successfully complete the Bar Examination and are not eligible (except in the limited circumstances described in the previous chapter) to enrol on the Vocational Course. Courses aimed at preparing candidates for the Bar Examination are no longer held at the Inns of Court School of Law, but are available at a number of other institutions.

This chapter describes first the Vocational Course and then goes on to describe the format of the Bar Examination.

The Vocational Course

The emphasis of the course is on a practical training in the specialist skills required by barristers with the aim of ensuring competence in those skills which barristers use in practice. This is achieved through the practice of skills in the tasks most commonly performed by junior members of the Bar during the early years of practice. The majority of class contact time is devoted to learning skills. The novel nature of this programme of study has led the Council of Legal Education, in conjunction with Blackstone Press, to publish a series of manuals. These are provided for every student on the course, but they are also on general sale in legal bookshops.

Skills training

There are short introductory courses intended to develop an awareness of the importance of interpersonal skills and written skills, for the barrister. These courses are completed during the first two weeks of the autumn term and form the foundation for the detailed teaching of the skills which have been identified as relevant to those practising at the Bar. These skills are: legal research, fact management, opinion writing, interviewing in conference, negotiating, drafting and advocacy. These separate skills courses vary in length – some are very short, for example the course on conference skills takes only three hours, whilst others which involve a wide range of techniques are comparatively long, for example the drafting course consists of twenty-six hours of class contact time. Each of these barrister skills is taught initially in a separate course. Students are then encouraged to use the skills acquired in combination with one another in the realistic context of sets of papers of a kind and level of complexity which a junior barrister could be expected to receive during the very early years of practice. These practical training exercises form a major element of the course.

Teaching methods

Students learn skills by gaining experience of them in interactive classes and through dealing with realistic sets of case papers. Role play is thus a central part of the learning process. Students will interview one another, role playing the barrister, the lay and/or professional client, negotiate solutions to legal problems with one another as a barrister might, draft documents and pleadings as required, conduct cases in 'courts' and 'tribunals' both as barristers and as others in the trial process, carry out legal research using original source materials and practitioners' works, write opinions on the merits of a case, on quantum and on the evidence, and experience how to sort out a set of papers identifying facts available and those which are required, how they are to be proved and what inferences can be drawn; they will also practice developing and presenting a theory for the case and/or finding a solution to the problem presented.

The skills training is conducted in a very practical way. For most students, this will present a very different experience from that provided at the academic stage of training. In practice, following instructions and finding and sorting out facts and how to use them, are all skills of crucial importance, whereas the ability to write an academic essay on a point of law is of much less value. As students progress through the course and become competent in each skill, the papers presented will become more and more complex, requiring the use of all the skills outlined above in the way in which these would combine together in practice.

Legal knowledge in the context of skills training
The practical work will be based largely on the 'core legal subjects' studied as part of the academic stage of training. Sets of papers may include legal issues related to, for example, the law of contract, or the law of tort. In addition, during the early part of the course, students will acquire a detailed knowledge of adjectival law (that is evidence, civil and criminal litigation), areas which will be of very great importance in carrying out the practical case work. In the third term, students will be given the opportunity to specialize in one of three fields of practice (namely general practice, chancery practice or commercial practice) in which it is expected that the second six months' pupillage will be spent. In this part of the course the practical work concentrates on the kinds of task which a second six month pupil is likely to undertake in two areas of law which are a usual part of practice in the chosen field. Preparation for practice here is aimed at the second six months of pupillage, because this is the first opportunity which the pupil will have to practise independently on his/her feet, and so experience and understanding of the tasks likely to be encountered is a valuable mechanism for building up confidence and competence.

Preparation for pupillage
Finally, in the last weeks of the third term there is a short course to help prepare students for pupillage.

Legal knowledge on the Vocational Course

The overall aim is largely to build on the knowledge which has been acquired at the academic stage of training in such a way as to prepare students for practice rather than to extend knowledge purely for its own sake. The whole emphasis is therefore to encourage students to discover the knowledge which is needed to resolve a particular case for themselves and then to use that knowledge efficiently and effectively for that purpose. In simulating practice, students are encouraged to become used to the idea of being independent and in control of their own professional lives.

The legal knowledge required on the course can be divided into four areas:

That of which the barrister should have a detailed knowledge and understanding

The rules of evidence, civil litigation, criminal litigation, and the rules of professional conduct are crucial to a successful practice. Concentrated courses of study are provided in the earlier part of the course in these areas.

That of which every barrister should have a general understanding

Barristers need to be able to recognize all the consequences of particular courses of action (that is, all the remedies which could be appropriate in a particular case; sentencing practice and procedure; the potential and growing impact of European community law; the basic structure and impact of the taxation system; an ability to read and understand basic accounts; and recognition of the legal ramifications of the different forms of business association). Short courses of study are provided for each of these areas.

That of which every barrister should have an overview

This knowledge is required because either it may influence the way in which a case is being conducted (so the potential impact of social security law, the European Convention on Human Rights, conflict of laws, the law of succession and legal aid is included), or because it is such a common field of practice for the junior practitioner that some awareness of the legal area is necessary (that is, landlord and tenant law, family law and sale of goods and consumer credit law). Again short courses of study are provided for each of these areas.

That which the barrister should know about two specialist areas of law and procedure before embarking on the second six months' of pupillage

These currently include: in the field of general practice, two specialist areas of law and procedure chosen from family law, employment law, sale of goods and consumer credit, and landlord and tenant in the field of chancery practice, two specialist areas of law and procedure chosen from trusts, tax and wills, conveyancing and real property and landlord and tenant; in the field of commercial practice. European Community law, the law of international trade, and sale of goods. It is anticipated that company law will be added in the near future.

The assessment process

The whole thrust of the assessment process is to reduce the amount of rote learning which students have traditionally been required to do and to require students to commit to memory only such principles and rules as are deemed absolutely necessary for successful practice. Hence in adjectival law, where a detailed knowledge of legal principle and/or procedure is required, multiple choice tests are held to establish that students have acquired that knowledge to the requisite standard.

In so far as the assessment of skills is concerned the purpose is to establish whether a student has reached, at the very least, a competent standard in the skills which will be used in the second six months' pupillage and is capable of using legal principles and rules in a practical way. Assessments in skills are held both during the course (the in-course assessments) and at its end (the final assessment). In order to ensure that students recognize that the skills assessment process is intended to judge whether students can perform the skills which a barrister needs in practice and are not intended to test a student's memory of the law, students are allowed to use any materials provided for them during the course. Students will be assessed on how they prepare for and carry out a number of tasks so, for example, in an advocacy assessment, students will be judged on their competence as an advocate, not on their ability to remember and restate a number of theories of what makes a great advocate. Assessment criteria are specified for each assessment and so students will know what the assessors are looking for in the case.

The involvement of the Bar

Practising barristers play a considerable part in the teaching and assessing of skills on the Vocational Course and have given wholehearted support to the development of the new curriculum, the authorship of materials and the preparation of sets of case papers.

The Bar Examination

The Bar Examination will continue in the same format as before for those who do not intend to practise as a barrister in any member state of the

European Community and students will be able to sit for the examination at Trinity and Michaelmas in each year.

The examination consists of six papers: general paper I (involving the law of tort and criminal law), general paper II (involving the law of contract and equity and trusts), evidence, civil and criminal procedure and two optional papers chosen from the following: revenue law, family law (and procedure), law of landlord and tenant, sale of goods and credit, local government and planning law, practical conveyancing, conflict of laws, labour law and social security law, the law of international trade, European community law and human rights. In choosing which of these optional papers to take, students are not entitled to repeat subjects previously studied as part of a degree course.

The syllabus and recommended reading lists for these papers are published each year in the Calendar. This can be purchased from the Inns of Court School of Law, as can examination papers from earlier years.

All the papers require a practical approach to be displayed, rather than an academic one. The papers require students to write opinions on the merits of the case and to give advice on matters of evidence and procedure and, where appropriate, sentence or quantum of damages, and to draft documents. Practice at these skills is crucial to success in the examination.

Pupillage and the practical training

DAVID LATHAM QC

David Latham is a QC practising in general common law in London. The former chairman of the Bar's working party on pupillage which reported in 1988, he is currently the Vice-Chairman of the Professional Standards Committee of the Bar Council.

Pupillage is the process by which the skills learnt in the vocational stage, and the law learnt at the academic stage are translated into practice. It is an exhilarating and painful experience. Exhilarating because there is no doubt that meeting real problems for the first time is rewarding, and the learning curve, however well the pupil has been prepared by both the academic and vocational stages, is steep. First appearances in court can be bruising. Not only is the pupil learning, but he or she is being constantly assessed to determine whether or not he or she is of barrister material, but also if he or she could be good enough to be taken on as a tenant in chambers at the end of pupillage.

The great strength of pupillage as a system is the relationship between the pupil and the pupil master. What may appear daunting in prospect is usually made not only acceptable but fun and enjoyable in practice by the support and help given by the pupil master. Whatever criticisms have been made about pupillage by those who have just been through it, the heartening message is that pupil masters have been conscientious and helpful.

The essence of pupillage is this close relationship between pupil master and pupil which enables the pupil to put the necessary skills into practice in three distinct stages: first by watching the way the pupil master works, this is by example; second by being able to practise the skills other than advocacy, such as pleading and advising, in circumstances where they can be monitored by the pupil master; third by being able to commence advocacy supported by the pupil master. Like any generalization, this does not reflect the course of every pupillage, particularly specialist pupillage, such as crime, where advocacy will be the overriding concern, or many chancery pupillages where the opportunity for advocacy may be infrequent. The great benefit of the system is that a very large proportion of learning process occurs more through a process of osmosis than by formal instruction.

Until 1988 there was little by way of control. The system had grown up and the Bar was small, and there was little if any need for formality. During the course of the overall review of training for the Bar it became apparent that the system should be improved, and the deficiencies inherent in any relatively unstructured training system (however successful in practice) have been dealt with by some relatively simple, but significant, changes. Pupil masters, who have to be approved, are now registered on a central register and pupils, when commencing pupillage, register as pupils to a particular pupil master. At the end of the first six months, the pupil master is required to sign a certificate indicating that the pupil has completed six months' pupillage satisfactorily, in which event the pupil will in turn receive his or her practising certificate. Until such time as the Bar Council receives the pupil master's certificate, the pupil is not entitled to appear in court or accept instructions on his or her own behalf. At the end of the second six months, a similar process of certification occurs. The result is a full certificate for the pupil, who is thereafter entitled to practise entirely on his or her own account. Each chambers is required to provide the pupils with a check list of the basic syllabus which the chambers considers to be appropriate for the particular type of work in which it is engaged. The check list can either be what might be called a proforma check list provided by the Bar Council or through the specialist Bar Associations, or an individual check list for the particular set of chambers, which has been approved by the Bar Council. In this way, it is hoped that both pupil and pupil master can monitor the progress of pupillage, so as to ensure that all relevant topics have been covered; at the end of pupillage, the completed check list provides a record of the experience gained by each pupil. Barristers have always undergone continuing professional education but a working party is currently devising a more structured system to ensure the continuation of the learning process during pupillage.

Payment to pupils? Ten years ago the Bar would have looked with surprise at anybody who had suggested such a thing. Apart from scholarships given by the Inns to the bright and the poor, pupillage was considered to be a privilege: indeed twenty years ago the pupil paid for that privilege. But in the last ten years things have changed dramatically. By five years ago, a significant number of chambers were providing modest awards out of their own funds. This has now progressed, not only under the stimulus of competition for the best graduate talent, but also within the Bar for the best students. The result is

that most chambers now offering pupillage also offer financing support for some or all of their pupils. The amount of this support has been increased each year so that some commercial sets are now offering up to £18,000 for the pupillage year, and ordinary common law sets are seeking to provide that which the Bar Council recommends, which is at least £6,000 either by way of awards, or by way of guaranteed earnings, during the pupillage year. In some sets of chambers, the latter is an attractive option, because pupils can earn quite significant sums of money during their second six months of pupillage. The speed with which things change can be gauged by the fact that, during the course of last year, the working party set up by the Bar Council to consider the whole question of finance for pupils, interviewed almost every set of chambers. It received firm promises of about 400 places for both the first and second six months of pupillage, the former funded to the tune of at least £3,000 each and the latter guaranteeing an income of a similar sum. While pupils are still expected to try and find their own pupillages, the new Bar Council computer called PATRIC is able to match those not fortunate enough to find their own places with the available vacancies. PATRIC also generates the contents of the Chambers, Pupillages and Awards Handbook which gives details of everything on offer, including mini-pupillages. Finance during the pupillage year should not be seen as a deterrent to those of the requisite ability who wish to come to the Bar.

At the same time as seeking to improve the quality of pupillage for those wishing to practise in independent practice at the Bar, the Bar has significantly improved the process of training for those barristers who wish to enter employment as barristers. All now have to complete six months' pupillage in chambers but the second six months can be served with an employed pupil master. This has enabled the Crown Prosecution Service, the Government Legal Service, the armed forces, and private industry to put forward training programmes which have received the approval of the Bar Council, and which provide a great variety of opportunities. In many instances, these schemes involve payment to the pupil, not only for the period spent with the employed pupil master, but also for the period in chambers.

Part VI
The qualified career

The Criminal Bar

Members of the Criminal Bar spend most of their professional lives engaged in court work. The life of a typical junior will entail travelling from court to court appearing in a succession of cases. At the start of his/her career, the criminal practitioner will appear most frequently in the magistrates' courts, progressing to cases in the crown courts as he/she gains greater experience. Preparation for cases largely has to be done in the evenings, as the day is taken up by travelling, waiting and appearing in court. Occasionally, because instructions will have been received late in the day or returned by another member of the Bar, a case may have to be prepared in the evening for the hearing the next day. Most members of the Criminal Bar both prosecute and defend rather than specializing specifically in either prosecution or defence work.

Typically, most members of chambers are out at court during the day and return in the late afternoon for conferences, and to collect papers and briefs. This enables pupils both to hear how more experienced practitioners deal with situations in general and to join in discussion about the type of case which they may have dealt with for the first time that day.

The rates of pay and procedures for paying fees have improved enormously, which now results in pupils earning sums which should at least cover their living expenses towards the end of their pupillage. Pupils normally can expect to earn fees during the second six months' pupillage as pupils in criminal chambers frequently obtain cases in their own right during the period. Academic achievement is clearly welcomed at the Criminal Bar, but the hallmark of the criminal practitioner is common sense, robustness and a fluent court manner.

The criminal barrister exercises judgement on the evidence and the law in advising clients on their plea (if defending) or on whether or not to proceed (when prosecuting). When defending, any plea tendered must be the plea of a defendant freely entered although it is proper for the barrister to tender robust advice if the circumstances warrant it.

It is becoming common for senior members of the Criminal Bar, whether QCs or juniors, to sit as assistant recorders trying criminal cases.

The Family Law Bar

Family law work covers a wide spectrum of work involving disputes between individuals which arise in the context of their domestic relations, and disputes relating to children.

The largest area of work concerns property and financial provision following divorce, and custody and/or access to children. Other work includes: provision for spouses and former spouses under the Inheritance Act 1985, where no provision has been made by the other spouse; divorce, judicial separation, nullity, recognition of foreign marriages; maintenance orders protection orders, child care proceedings. It involves also a knowledge of other complex areas of law including tax and foreign marriage law. Increasingly, cases are being taken to the European Court of Human Rights.

Family law work can be practised exclusively but is often combined with a general common law and/or criminal practice.

Non-litigious work involves the drafting of pleadings and affidavits and advisory work.

The work is rewarding because of the deep human problems which are encountered. However, it requires patience and special skills as the family practitioner has to act as counsellor and conciliator as well as advocate.

The Chancery Bar

The Chancery Bar consists of those barristers who practise principally in the Chancery Division of the High Court. The work covers a wide variety of areas of practice whose common theme is 'property'. No two chancery practices are the same and emphases differ widely.

A general chancery practitioner may find himself doing any (or all) of the following: trusts; revenue – including especially inheritance tax; charities; company work; partnerships and other business arrangements (these may be of many sorts and most of them could well be described as 'commercial'); insolvency; land – including particularly the sale of land and interests in land such as rights of way and covenants; landlord and tenant including business tenancies and agricultural holdings; town and country planning (though rather less of this); probate, including contested probate of wills, family provision and the administration of estates; court of protection; mortgages and other commercial securities; many commercial matters with a property/money/ banking element.

There are some tighter degrees of specialization; thus, there are chambers who do predominantly company and insolvency work and others which specialize in landlord and tenant work. There are pure revenue specialists and patents specialists. Most chancery chambers have particular 'house' specializations.

The chancery practitioners appear in court far more than they once did, although the amount of time which any individual practitioner spends in court will vary.

The majority of chancery sets are in London but it is perfectly possible to be a chancery practitioner in the larger provincial areas.

The work undertaken by the Chancery Bar is of a demanding nature, requiring academic aptitude and the ability to express oneself clearly in writing as well as orally. Each set has its own entry requirements but, as a general guide, no serious entrant ought to have less than a good honours degree, ie at least upper second.

The prospects for success are good, both in terms of monetary reward and job satisfaction. As a general indication, whilst beginners in their first year cannot expect to make much profit, after ten years earnings of between £40,000 and £50,000 net per annum can be expected.

The Revenue Bar

Revenue work is substantially advisory and comprises such areas of work as how to minimize the taxation of proposed transactions and the taxation consequences of transactions which have already taken place.

Practitioners therefore work in: income tax, corporation tax, capital gains tax, value added tax, inheritance tax, stamp duty and capital duty, and/or petroleum revenue tax.

In respect of income tax a significant element of work involves the resolution of liabilities where there has been under-declaration in the past.

Practitioners, for the most part, do not often become involved in a great deal of litigation in court. They do however appear from time to time before the General Commissioners and the Special Commissioners of the Inland Revenue.

The Revenue Bar Association has approximately sixty members of whom about fifty practise in all or most of the areas mentioned above; the remainder practise in a specific area in conjunction with the use of their expertise in another field, for example a specialist in inheritance tax might also specialize in chancery work.

The London Common Law and Commercial Bar

The members of the London Common Law and Commercial Bar Association practise in such widely diverse fields as admiralty, landlord and tenant, local government and parliamentary work. Any description of the work of barristers in the Association can only be in very general terms.

The focus of many practitioners' work is litigation in disputes concerning contractual or tortious questions in the Queen's Bench Division (including the commercial and admiralty courts and the official referees' courts) and, particularly for more junior barristers, in the county courts. The work includes cases concerning personal injuries, nuisance, sales of goods, sales of shares and businesses, banking and professional negligence. This work is often combined with specialization in other areas such as employment law, administrative law, defamation and construction law.

As the name of the Association indicates, many of its members also practise wholly or mainly at the Commercial Bar; the principal subjects of commercial work are international trade, shipping, insurance and banking. These areas of law often concern international disputes, with litigation not only in the courts, but by way of arbitration in London or elsewhere.

Although the majority of the work of members of the Association concerns litigation in one way or another – whether it be an appearance at trial or a pre-trial hearing, the drafting of pleadings or the giving of advice – the Common Law Bar also provides a more general advisory service to business and other clients and assists in drafting terms of business, agreements and other non-litigious documents. The work of the Common Law Bar also includes appearances at a wide variety of standing and *ad hoc* tribunals and enquiries.

The Commercial Bar Association (COMBAR)

The Commercial Bar Association (COMBAR) is composed of commercial chambers and individual practitioners at the Commercial Bar.

The Commercial Bar primarily services the specialist legal needs of the City of London, particularly international commercial litigation and arbitration. It gives advice to clients from all over the world, reflecting the importance of London as an international commercial and financial centre and as a forum for the resolution of international disputes.

Its principal fields of practice are: international trade, shipping and aviation, banking and financial services, insurance and reinsurance, commodity transactions, insolvency, mergers and acquisitions, competition law, intellectual property, professional negligence, licensing, judicial review of governmental acts, employment, European Community matters and public international law.

Some of the particular services offered by members of COMBAR are:

(a) acceptance of direct instructions from overseas lawyers and other professional advisers

(b) advice on legal matters and disputes and other matters arising anywhere in the world

(c) acting as advocates in overseas courts and tribunals of the European Community, Singapore, Hong Kong, Malaysia, Caribbean Islands, Bermuda and elsewhere

(d) acting as advocates in international arbitrations in England or elsewhere – more international and commercial arbitration takes place in London than in any other city in the world

(e) giving evidence as an expert on English law in courts or arbitrations elsewhere in the world.

The Patent Bar

Practitioners at the Patent Bar do not deal with patent matters alone. They are generally specialists in all kinds of intellectual property law including the law of patents, registered designs, copyright, trade marks and passing off. Many practitioners also specialize in the law of breach of confidence, which has much in common with more orthodox intellectual property.

The work inevitably requires the practitioner to grasp matters of technical and scientific complexity which require an aptitude for scientific problems. The vast majority of practitioners in this field therefore have some form of scientific qualification, and/or scientific experience. Such qualifications may well be a significant factor in the recruitment of pupils.

By the very nature of intellectual property, much litigation involves applications for interlocutory injunctions in the High Court, such work often being done by junior barristers. A great deal of time also is taken up with paperwork for, as a specialist adviser, a practitioner will be heavily involved in the preparation for such applications. As practitioners become more senior, they will do less interlocutory work, and take on more full actions, which can be extremely complex and lengthy.

In addition to High Court work, the patent practitioner appears also at hearings in the Patent Office and the Trade Marks Registry.

On the non-litigious side, advice may be sought on potential patent, trademark and copyright infringements, the question of validity of patents and trademarks and the drafting of licensing agreements. Questions of European law may well arise in this context and practitioners should have at least a working knowledge of the competition provisions of the Treaty of Rome.

Patent practitioners also are increasingly being asked to advise in highly technical contractual disputes, particularly those involving computer technology.

Patent practitioners are entitled to take instructions directly from patent and trademark agents as well as from solicitors.

The Administrative Law Bar

Members of the Bar practising in administrative law are concerned with applications for judicial review in the High Court and appearances before tribunals and enquiries. Judicial review is concerned with the body of general principles which govern the exercise of powers and duties by public authorities in many fields.

Local government, immigration (including habeas corpus and extradition), housing, homeless persons, town and country planning, education, social security, employment and licensing are all topics which figure prominently in the case law on the subject. Recently there have been a number of applications by companies in commercial and tax areas. In the last few years there have been important judicial review decisions involving local authorities concerning rating and budgetary policy. Applications for judicial review can be made in both civil and criminal matters.

Examples of public bodies that have been challenged include government departments such as DHSS, defence and foreign and commonwealth affairs, and local government activities such as area and district health, local housing and police authorities. Also courts and tribunals involved include the High Court, the Immigration Appeal Tribunal and the Prison Board of Governors. Domestic and professional bodies include the Professional Conduct Committees of the Law Society and the Bar. Public corporations and other regulatory bodies include the BBC and London Regional Transport. Applications also have been made against educational institutions including universities and school governors.

Town and country planning and supplementary benefits are the two main areas of the law relating to public administration which involve preparation for and attendance at tribunals and enquiries. Types of tribunals include rent tribunals, local valuation courts (rating), mental health review tribunals and family practitioners committees.

The Local Government and Planning Bar

The work of the Local Government and Planning Bar principally concerns disputes with or relating to public authorities, which are mainly but not exclusively local authorities. Most, but not all, of these disputes relate in some way to land. The areas most commonly covered include town and country planning, compulsory purchase, highways, rating, housing and the general administration of local government. There is a significant amount of advisory work.

As far as the advocacy side of the work is concerned, much of it is undertaken at public enquiries, of which planning enquiries are the most common type. Appearances are also required in courts at all levels including the High Court and the Lands Tribunal.

There are not a great number of specialist practitioners in this field, probably in the region of 120 regulars. This roughly corresponds with the number of the Local Government and Planning Bar. Most are members of specialist sets of chambers in London which deal with this type of work. Also there are a number of individuals who have expert knowledge in this area but practise also in general common law or other areas.

Some of the work falls squarely into the wider field of 'administrative law'. There is also an overlap in the sense that some practitioners at the Local Government and Planning Bar regularly do other work in more or less related fields. An interesting example perhaps is that most of the members of the Parliamentary Bar, whose work includes the promotion of or opposition to private and local bills before parliamentary committees, are also practitioners at the Local Government and Planning Bar.

Official Referees and the Bar

The construction industry (taking building and engineering together) is by most criteria the largest single industrial activity in the United Kingdom economy, and is extensively employed abroad. It is served by the large and well organized professions of architects, engineers and surveyors, and by specialist solicitors and barristers.

Construction contracts are complicated and disputes are frequent. Many of these disputes are resolved by arbitrators, but an ever-increasing number are tried by official referees. There are up to ten official referees' courts, which are part of the High Court, sitting at the Royal Courts of Justice.

The official referees have their unusual title because they used to have cases 'referred' to them by judges of the High Court, perhaps for a report on matters of detail such as accountancy or surveying evidence. Nowadays they are specialist judges in their own right and try almost all the construction cases in the High Court.

There are perhaps sixty or seventy barristers who confine their work almost entirely to construction cases (the Construction Bar) and a considerably larger number of members of the Bar who appear in such cases fairly frequently and could be said to be specialists. The Construction Bar as such is largely concentrated in two sets of chambers.

Work at the 'Construction Bar' is arduous by reason of the size and complexity of the cases and much of the work is done before arbitrators. There is overseas work, particularly for QCs. The rewards can be great. Official referees are generally appointed from QCs who have already achieved distinction in other fields.

Members of the Construction Bar frequently also have professional qualifications as surveyors or engineers. Potential practitioners in this field should consider carefully whether to commence their career elsewhere; for example in industry, or as barristers practising in common law chambers.

Barristers in commerce, finance and industry

DAVID FLETCHER ROGERS

David Fletcher Rogers is a Barrister and was the proposer and joint founder of the Bar Association for Commerce, Finance and Industry. His career has largely been as a member of a legal department of one of the great British companies with subsidiaries worldwide.

For many years barristers have been employed as in-house counsel who are recognized as important members of the management team of important companies.

The contrast between private practice and in-house work

The most important difference is that the in-house lawyers generally do positive legal work – it can be the formation of profitable companies, the licensing of inventions for royalty, creation of joint ventures, projects which will lead to employment opportunities. The private practitioner will find that the work is often concerned with the negative side of life, damages for injuries, dealing with criminals, disputes as to housing. All very necessary but much better if the problems had not arisen. Many find this type of work upsetting such as Sir Robin Day, though this was but one reason for his departure to the media.

What barristers in business do

Naturally, one of the main ways in which barristers (both men and women) employed in business use their knowledge of the law is as staff legal advisers to companies or other organizations. In one way or another the law affects every part of a company's activities – from finance and mergers to the protection of patents and trademarks and international trade. With increasing legislation particularly with regard to industrial relations and EEC law, management relies more and more on the advice of the trained lawyer.

Increasingly, barristers are rising to the most senior managerial appointments in industry and a legal qualification offers an excellent avenue to a directorship to those lawyers who are prepared to broaden the horizons of their knowledge and acquire a thorough grasp of business techniques and methods. Lawyers occupy posts such as chairman, managing director, director and company secretary in commercial, financial and industrial organizations and thus their career structure is not confined solely to membership of legal departments.

So the job of the barrister in business is both important and full of interest. Whenever new developments in the company are being planned his/her advice will be sought at an early stage. In the course of one week a barrister might be found advising on a new form of contract, sitting in at a conference to discuss expansion plans and travelling overseas to advise a foreign subsidiary company or to negotiate a contract with a customer. Even at the beginning of his/her career they will usually enjoy an overall view of the company's operations and may well be asked to advise at board-level, helping to influence decisions rather than merely executing them.

Your choice of career

If you decide to become a lawyer, you have two choices before you. You can become a barrister or solicitor; and in either case you can go into private practice, or you can choose to make your career in business, the civil service or local government.

In making these choices, you may find it useful to bear in mind the following factors among others.

To make a successful legal career in commerce, finance or industry you need to develop three qualities in particular:

- Clarity of thought, with the ability to 'see the wood for the trees' in a complex situation, and to find a practical solution to any legal problem which is disclosed as a result. The process of studying law itself helps to develop this quality.
- A good commercial sense, so that you can advise on the best course of action within the law to achieve the business objectives in view.
- In many jobs, the ability to negotiate business deals as well as to advise on their legal implications.

The work done by barristers and solicitors in employment is very similar, and many employers do not distinguish between the two branches of the profession when recruiting for legal appointments. There are a few restrictions on the work which a barrister can do, thus he cannot generally appear in the High Court on behalf of his employers, but businesses do not require lawyers on their staff for such a purpose – though increasingly barristers are required to represent employers at bodies such as industrial tribunals which are open to barristers in employment, they can also appear for their employers in the magistrates and county courts.

In 1990 barristers were for the first time permitted to work as employees of other disciplines such as accountants, solicitors and the like, and many now do so. Some also work as part-time independent in-house counsel. Such work can be very attractive to a barrister with young children and who does not wish to work full-time.

The great tradition of the Bar of England and Wales, and membership of an Inn of Court – carrying with it the opportunity of meeting and conversing with experienced members of the Bar over lunch or dinner in the Hall of the Inn – have an attraction for many prospective lawyers.

Pupillage

A barrister is not allowed to practise on his own at the Bar until he has served as a pupil of a practising barrister for at least twelve months although he can appear in court and earn fees himself during the second six months of his pupillage.

A barrister taking a position in business need not have served a pupillage although some employers consider the experience gained as a pupil to be an advantage, indeed from a barrister's own point of view it is desirable that he undergoes pupillage.

Commercial pupils

Some legal departments offer a scheme whereby barristers are taken on as pupils in order to give them training in the ways of industry, but these opportunities are comparatively few and eagerly sought.

The Bar Association for Commerce, Finance and Industry (BACFI)

This was founded in 1965 and is the association for those barristers in business. It is very active in enhancing the position of the business barrister and BACFI has representatives on the Bar Counsel Benchers of the Inns of Court and other legal bodies. BACFI is also prominent in law reform.

One of its functions is to help barristers get started in business as well as make them aware of job opportunities. At present there is a great demand for competent lawyers in industry with the ever increasing amount of new law in the form of Acts of Parliament, EEC Directives, Regulations and Codes of Practice.

To find out about these appointments one should write to The Secretary, BACFI, 2 Plowden Buildings, Middle Temple Lane, London EC4Y 9AT.

What jobs are available to the newly qualified?

It may be a little difficult to get a job straight from pupillage as employers tend to ask for people of experience.

This is where BACFI can be especially helpful; they keep a record of those companies which may take recently qualified people as well as those who have had a commercial pupillage. There is always a great opportunity for all newly qualified to show ability and initiative.

Anyone thinking of going into commerce as a lawyer should write to some of the companies with large legal departments to see if there is a vacant job in the department, doing anything.

Companies like people to show initiative, and many companies take on students or newly qualified lawyers during the summer months. The work one does will be rather routine but it will give you and the legal department an opportunity of judging whether you are suited to working in commercial surroundings.

One such lawyer is now head of an important department in one of the more successful merchant and investment banks known as 3i. She started as a clerk to a solicitor's clerk even though a barrister, because they would not take her on as a lawyer. It was not long before her own ability cleared her from that occupation to one of giving legal advice.

What are the qualities for a successful lawyer in industry?

He or she must have good ability coupled with common sense – the ability to distinguish between worthwhile points and others. It is also essential to have the type of personality whereby you get on with people at all levels.

People must learn to have confidence in you, this means when a mistake is made you admit it and do not cover it up.

You must be master of your subject area. In business there are a wide range of legal topics, some needing their own special knowledge and skills such as industrial relations, copyright, patents, commercial contracts, turnkey projects, health and safety at work, competition law including EEC, licensing trademarks, company law and many others, including some as interesting as anti counterfeiting work.

The successful lawyer will be a specialist in some few areas, and must be able to recognize when a problem arises outside his speciality in order to refer it to a colleague.

Contrast the position of the barrister in private practice who by and large does negative legal work, such as seeking damages for injury, husbands or wives desperate for divorce, remedies being sought for broken contracts and criminals to be jailed. All these events occur as a result of something going wrong. It is more satisfying for many to know that their contributions in practising law are constructive.

On the inside looking out

The in-house counsel knows at an early stage what is happening and is part of a project team from beginning to end. They may travel extensively, which for the younger person has attractions, and will become conversant in many cases with overseas law and developments. They must be forward looking and pro-active rather than reactive, that is to guide their employers to prevent trouble arising rather than dealing with the consequence of the employers going wrong – though of course this does occur.

An example is given of in-house lawyers who were well practised in EEC law long before the private practitioner, and were advising their companies as to how to deal with the new laws. The in house person also knows his employers business thoroughly which makes legal work so much more interesting.

Such is the complexity of present day law that the in-house lawyer will need to be in touch with private practitioners for specialized advice and over the years one builds up a relationship with the solicitors to one's employer which is very worthwhile for it is the function of the in-house lawyer to see that they are fully and adequately instructed.

Quality of the work and its rewards

It is very worthwhile. The rewards are good – a company secretary of a large industrial company will command a salary of over £50,000 with a car, plus in many cases bonuses and share options which are becoming increasingly popular and indeed can, and do, make people quite rich.

At the start, one's first job will be about £18–20,000 according to location. Promotion up the salary scale is swift because if a company has a good lawyer they know they must pay to keep them.

Once a lawyer has had two to three years industrial experience there should be no difficulty in moving to another post, as many do in their early years to gain experience.

There is now no discrimination against women, who have more and more opportunities to get to the top – Kodak Limited, for example, who appointed a woman as head of the legal division have since elected her to the board of that company.

Transferring from the Bar to the Law Society

Under the Qualified Lawyers Transfer Regulations 1990, a barrister wishing to qualify as a solicitor is required either to have served twelve months in pupillage and twelve months in legal practice acceptable to the Law Society, or two years in legal practice acceptable to the Law Society, or such period not exceeding two years as the Society may determine in a solicitor's office, employed in a way compatible with articles and pass the Professional Conduct and Accounts paper set in the Qualified Lawyers Transfer Test.

Each year some five hundred barristers transfer to become solicitors and this number is steadily rising.

Part VII
The directory

How to select a firm of solicitors

Articles of this type usually divide into two groups. There are those which give logical instructions leading to a conclusion about which there is little argument, and there are others which are not so clear cut and require subjective judgements. Unfortunately this article falls squarely into the latter category.

There are thousands of solicitors' firms in this country from which to choose and probably the best approach is to consider a list of questions. This enables you to establish the criteria for an acceptable firm and so to narrow down the choice. The questions vary depending on who you are: a businessman who wants to retain a firm, a student who wishes to train with one, or a qualified solicitor changing firms or moving back into practice.

The businessman

To the businessman the Law Society operating through its local branches is able to offer a great deal of guidance and advice. This support can perhaps be complemented by a list of questions:

(a) Where must the firm have offices? How far away can your main contact office be from your premises, and do you have other plants, sites or branches around the country which need offices near them?

(b) Do you need a firm with a large international office network or with representation in a particular continent or country, or is your business really only in the UK?

(c) Does your business have any especially complicated or obscure aspects which might require the firm retained to have a particular skill or expertise?

(d) Do you want to retain a firm as general legal advisers, or do you also wish it to possess specialist departments?

(e) Will the character or size of your business change in the near future? If so, what extra requirements will arise?

(f) What type of firm do your competitors use and why?

(g) What type of firm do your other advisers (eg banker, auditor etc) recommend?

(h) Do you have any personal experience of or connection with any firms?

Having used this list to obtain a manageable number of practices, it is then quite acceptable to visit each in turn and discuss your needs with a partner. This enables you to gain a first impression and the discussions are always useful. More than one may have to exclude itself from consideration for a range of possible ethical and practical reasons, and partners are also quite open if they feel you would be more suited to another firm. Their aim is to build a long-term relationship – a brief and uncomfortable one serves nobody's interests. Ultimately, however, the choice must be the firm with which you feel most at ease. You will have to share much confidential information and rely on the partner's advice, and therefore trust and a common viewpoint are essential for both parties.

The potential trainee solicitor

The student or school-leaver reading this part of the guide is in a rather different position. 'Articles', the period when you add practical training and experience to the theory you have learnt, are available in many different places – in local government, industry and commerce, magistrates' courts and a few law centres. However, because the majority take articles in private practice, this section is addressed at them, though little changes for those considering other paths to admission to the Roll of Solicitors. You have three main requirements. You want a good training leading as painlessly as possible to qualification, a wide variety of work experience to ensure a good development of your professional skills, and finally, an interesting working life in a pleasant environment.

The first requirement is very seldom a problem as the Law Society keeps a close watch on the calibre of training offered by firms to their trainee solicitors and the firms themselves have every incentive to support you. The second two are more subjective in that different people prefer different types of practice. Once again, a list of questions may help to crystallize your thoughts and narrow the choice.

(a) Where do you wish to train? Do you want the office to be near your home, school, university or polytechnic, or do you wish to live and work somewhere new?

(b) What size of firm do you want to work for? Large firms say they offer a comprehensive array of national and international resources and opportunities. Medium sized ones claim to give the trainee solicitor all that he or she can benefit from, usually with a range of national and international links, while still not losing the personal touch. Small firms consider that they alone offer a personal and almost continuous training, with far greater client involvement and daily contact with the partners. Whichever appeals to you, of more relevance is the size of office.

(c) What kind of training package do you want? Various types are available, with each firm offering different mixes and amounts of in-house classes and seminars on professional and managerial skills.

(d) What type of client work interests you? While solicitors will turn their hands to most things at the request of clients, it is still true that certain firms consider themselves specialists in particular types of business. Such specialization may be more evident at an office level. Thus, a firm's Central London office is likely to have more service sector clients and fewer manufacturers than an office of the same firm in the Midlands, and a large City practice is likely to place heavy emphasis on company commercial work. There is a similar choice to be made about the size of client you would prefer. Large organizations tend to retain similar sized firms. If you join a partnership with a portfolio of such clients, you will inevitably deal with their problems. However, a smaller firm could say – with some fairness – that you seldom see the full picture and become a cog in the machine, and may not work with the same people again. They would instead offer earlier responsibility and greater work continuity, though with fewer of your clients making the front page of *The Times*.

(e) When do you wish to join a firm? Not all can be flexible.

(f) What is a firm's overtime policy for trainee solicitors?

(g) Do you want to join a specialist department? Some firms offer the option of training in specialist departments from the start.

(h) Looking ahead to the day you qualify, what do you think you would then like to do? It would obviously be best if you chose initially to stay in practice, for you to be able to continue your career without having to change firms.

As for the businessman, this list of questions should enable you to reduce your choice to a few firms which can then be approached. Many offer open days and other informal contacts before you decide to make a formal application.

The qualified solicitor

Such a person may feel they need less guidance as to which firm to select. However, if only for completeness, set out below are a few thoughts which may help to make the choice clearer.

(a) Are you keen to work in a general practice or do you want to be a specialist and if so, of what kind? Some firms may not have the department of your choice or only a small one.

(b) Does your work experience have any glaring omissions you wish to fill, or does any aspect of it make you particularly attractive to a firm?

(c) What kind of salary package do you want, bearing in mind the cost of living in an area and its general desirability?

(d) What are the prospects for promotion and what level of responsibility are you looking for?

(e) Do you want the option of an overseas secondment or one to a client?

(f) What is a firm's attitude to staff who wish to change departments? Is it easy to move across to a different specialist unit or to go to a different office?

(g) What are your long-term aims, and how will your choice of firm affect their attainment?

With a steadily growing profession and buoyant economy, you will realize that you are in an enviable position. As a qualified solicitor, you represent a significant fee to an employment agency. To a firm, you are a member of staff who comes ready qualified and with experience. These are expensive to give staff, not to mention the time, administrative effort and wastage involved. As a result, it is assumed that you will apply to several firms and many use more than one employment agency. Finally, as a member of the Law Society, you can always discuss your position with them. While they obviously cannot recommend a particular firm, the staff are very helpful in other ways, as are the local law societies, for which contact details are given in the first part of the guide.

Using the directory

The following pages contain a directory representing a cross section of UK solicitors' firms, each of which has provided a comprehensive profile. A complete list of members and firms is published annually under the direction of the Law Society, and details of particular ones can be obtained from the local law societies.

The information given in the profiles is an amalgam of that most frequently requested by students, businessmen and members of the profession. Firms write their own entries, using a proforma, to ensure their accuracy. The information they supply is thus directly comparable. The only variations are a minor rewording of the line headings where this gives a more accurate picture (for example, some firms have senior rather than managing partners), and the omission of irrelevant lines (such as where a firm has no overseas offices). However, care must be taken when interpreting trainee solicitor salary figures. Predictions two years hence are of limited value, so many firms have indicated what they currently offer or looked forward only as far as 1992.

Some profiles are also accompanied by an advertisement. Partnerships have only recently begun publicizing themselves in this fashion and it is instructive to compare images of how they see and choose to project themselves.

The directory has been arranged in alphabetical order, and the writers were encouraged to try and convey the maximum possible factual information in the space available. This year thirty entries were submitted for inclusion and it is hoped to continue this growth in future editions, thereby adding to the usefulness of this part of the guide.

The Law Society Recruitment Service

The Law Society Recruitment Service is a free and confidential service to applicants, and experienced consultants will be happy to give you advice on any aspect of your career.

Qualified solicitors

Applicants seeking a move within the profession are invited to submit a comprehensive Curriculum Vitae or fill out a registration form (available from the office), returning it by post to a consultant at the address opposite.

You will then be contacted either by telephone, if permissible (discretion assured), or by letter to discuss your requirements in depth. If practical, we will also be happy to arrange a confidential chat at our offices. Based on our understanding of your requirements, your details will be forwarded to a selection of appropriate vacancies currently on our files, and we will then contact you when we have generated positive interest from a client. We will of course be happy to discuss specific vacancies before submitting your details, if this is preferred.

Trainee solicitors

The Law Society Recruitment Service publishes a free monthly list of vacancies for *Immediately Available* trainee solicitors, ie those who have completed, or who are about to complete their Law Society Finals. Telephone: 071-320 5940 for further details.

Equal opportunity policy

The Law Society Recruitment Service is committed to a policy of equal opportunities for all applicants irrespective of sex, race and disability.

Should you wish to discuss any aspects of the Service further, or to place a current vacancy, please contact the Manager, Murdoch Morrison.

THE LAW SOCIETY
RECRUITMENT SERVICE

The official Recruitment Service of the Law Society

227/228 The Strand
London
WC2R 1BA

Telephone 071-242 1222
DX56 Chancery Lane

THE LAW SOCIETY'S RECRUITMENT SERVICE is a response to the obvious need within the profession for a recruitment service which offers candidates career guidance and choice through the contacts and resources of the Law Society and offers firms the best aspects of the commercial agencies at a more reasonable price. The service is confidential to both firms and applicants.

Allen & Overy

Main office: 9 Cheapside, London EC2V 6AD. Tel: 071-248 9898; Fax: 071-236 2192.
Overseas offices: Brussels, Dubai, Hong Kong, Madrid, New York, Paris, Tokyo.
Senior partner: J M Kennedy.
Number of partners: 98 worldwide as at January 1991.
Number of professional staff: Over 500 worldwide.
Number of other staff: Over 500 worldwide.
Firm history: Founded in 1930, Allen & Overy is one of the largest firms in the country. With its main office in the City of London and a network of offices in all the world's financial centres, the practice has always concentrated on commercial work with a substantial international element.
Firm structure: While the practice is run on an efficient partnership model, more important to our success is the style of the firm. We enjoy our work and our aim is to serve our clients in the most progressive and effective way possible, whether this be through specifically tailored teams drawn from our pool of experts or the individual attention of a partner or other solicitor.
Major events in the past year: Important developments during 1990 included the opening of our office in Madrid further emphasizing Allen & Overy's commitment to an international practice.
Range of client services: The main areas of the firm's work are company and commercial (including international and domestic banking, corporate finance and bonds), litigation, property, private client, EEC and competition law and corporate taxation, with other specialist areas covering pensions, share incentives, employee benefits, intellectual property and construction.
Number of trainee solicitors required for 1993: Approximately 70.
Minimum academic requirements: Applications are welcomed from both law and non-law graduates. At least an upper second class degree standard is expected.
Starting salary: £16,000 per annum in September 1990.
Number of qualified solicitors required for 1991: We are always interested in applications from first-class qualified solicitors.
Starting salary: £25,000 per annum in September 1990.
Annual leave entitlement: 22 days plus bank holidays.
Professional development policies and programmes: In addition to our wide range of work of the highest quality, we can offer a first-class, structured training programme which continues after articles, with regular assessments and the advantages of the latest professional know-how and technical support systems.

Prospects for employment with the firm after articles are excellent: seventy-one of the present partners were articled with the firm.
For brochure and application form contact: A brochure 'Allen & Overy: Qualifying as a Solicitor' is available from the recruitment partner at the above address.

A Two-Way Process

It's not possible to define our ideal candidate because we're selecting people not CVs.

The people we're looking for will have certain qualities in common. They will have a good degree but not necessarily in law. They may be from any university or poly. They will be highly intelligent, questioning, motivated, thoughtful, self-aware – looking for a career that's both intellectually challenging and demanding.

Selecting aspiring lawyers for Allen & Overy is a two-way process. We're looking for our partners of the future: you're looking for a rewarding job which will stretch you and offer the highest standard of training. The right people will benefit both themselves and us. If, after reading this, you feel you might be one of them, get in touch with Gideon Hudson, Allen & Overy, 9 Cheapside, London EC2V 6AD. Tel: 071-248 9898.

ALLEN & OVERY

LONDON · BRUSSELS · DUBAI · HONG KONG · MADRID · NEW YORK · PARIS · TOKYO

CONTACT FORM

To: The Head of Recruitment

. . . .

. . . .

. . . .

THE IVANHOE GUIDE TO
THE LEGAL PROFESSION 1991

I have been interested to read about your organization in the above publication and would be grateful if you would send me a copy of your brochure and an application form.

Signed . . . . Date . . . .

*Name . . . .

*Address . . . .

. . . .

. . . .

*Please print

Argles & Court

Main office: 12 Mill Street, Maidstone, Kent ME15 6XU. Tel: 0622-757461; Fax: 0622-687266.

Other offices: Bearsted, Larkfield and Walderslade.

Senior partner: Raymond C Harris

Number of partners: 16

Number of staff: 160

Firm history: Argles & Court was founded in 1901 and has developed progressively over the last ninety years to achieve it's current position as one of the foremost practices in the South East. The firm is run upon departmental lines in common with most medium to large sized practices. As far as future development is concerned, the firm remains committed to further expansion, particularly in the areas of information technology and ensuring its ability to meet the challenge of 1992.

Range of client services: In the last ten years Argles & Court has concentrated its development on the law relating to company and business affairs and boasts a comprehensive commercial service for its clients. In addition, it maintains expertise in all other areas of the law, including private client, litigation, planning, matrimonial, probate and conveyancing.

Number of trainee solicitors required for 1993: 2

Minimum academic requirements: A minimum academic requirement of an upper second degree is desirable together with a pass in the Law Society Final exams.

Starting salary: The firm is committed to paying in excess of the established local Law Society minimum.

Professional development policies and programmes: Argles & Court devotes a great deal of effort to the training of all of its professional staff, thus ensuring they provide clients with the best possible advice.

For brochure and application form contact: Timothy J Bignell.

Ashurst Morris Crisp

Main office: Broadwalk House, 5 Appold Street, London EC2A 2HA. Tel: 071-638 1111; Telex: 887067; Fax: 071-972 7990.

Overseas links: Ashursts is the UK member of Le Club, an international association of major corporate law firms in Europe and the United States. The firm has recently opened offices in Brussels, Paris and Tokyo.

Senior partner: M G H Bell.

Number of partners: 43 plus 29 associates.

Number of other professional staff: 180

Number of other staff: 258

Firm history: Ashursts was founded in 1821 and has ranked among the leading City law firms throughout its history. Ashursts is currently fifth among English law firms for the number of corporate clients listed on The Stock Exchange and in the top three for the number of listed corporate clients per partner. Stock Exchange related transactions provide the single most important area of the firm's work.

Firm structure: The practice comprises four departments, these are: company, commercial and banking; property and planning; litigation; and tax.

Range of client services: Ashurst Morris Crisp draws nearly all its clients from the business sector. It provides a full range of services for corporate clients: acquisitions, disposals, corporate finance, banking, management buy-outs, tax, pensions, commercial property and litigation advice.

The firm's fundamental aim is to provide practical advice which resolves a client's problems.

Number of trainee solicitors required for 1993: 25 (recruited for 1992: 25)

Minimum academic requirements: The firm concentrates on recruiting people who have excellent academic ability and who it believes will be able to communicate and work easily with colleagues and clients. Both law and non-law graduates who have broad interests and a sense of humour are encouraged to apply.

Starting salary: £16,100 (1990) – under review.

Annual leave entitlement: 20 days.

Professional development policies and programmes: During articles a trainee solicitor undertakes practical training in those areas of law in which the firm practises. A trainee solicitor will spend time within three of the four main departments, normally directly supervised by a partner. Each trainee solicitor will experience a broad range of work in the department in which he or she sits during articles. The firm places great emphasis upon training and has an extensive training programme including regular seminars, know-how groups and skills training sessions for trainee solicitors and qualified solicitors.

Brochure available from: Edward Sparrow to whom applications should be made with a curriculum vitae.

Established in 1821, Ashursts has been one of the leading City law firms throughout the greater part of its history. Ashursts currently ranks fifth amongst English law firms for the number of corporate clients listed on The Stock Exchange and in the top three for the number of listed corporate clients per partner.

Stock Exchange related transactions provide the single most important area of the firm's work.

"No articled clerk will reach the end of articles without having created an impression and having established a reputation within the firm."

Over the years, Ashursts has developed its own style of operation. Great emphasis is placed internally on an informal atmosphere that allows rapid communication between all members of the firm. As part of that approach, the firm concentrates on recruiting people who have high academic ability and a sense of humour and who will be able to communicate and work easily with colleagues and clients.

A brochure may be obtained from your careers adviser or from Edward Sparrow at the address below.

ASHURST
MORRIS
CRISP

Broadwalk House, 5 Appold Street, London EC2A 2HA Telephone 071-638 1111
Telex 887067 Facsimile 071-972 7990 CDE Box number 639

THE IVANHOE GUIDES
ORDER FORM

Please supply the following Ivanhoe Guides:

- [ ] The Ivanhoe Guide to Pensions Management 1991   £6.95
- [ ] The Ivanhoe Guide to the Banking and Securities Industry 1991   £6.95
- [ ] The Ivanhoe Guide to Management Consultants 1991   £6.95
- [ ] The Ivanhoe Guide to Insurance 1991   £6.95
- [ ] The Ivanhoe Guide to Chartered Accountants 1991   £6.95
- [ ] The Ivanhoe Guide to Actuaries 1991   £6.95
- [ ] The Ivanhoe Guide to Chartered Patent Agents 1991   £6.95
- [ ] The Ivanhoe/Blackstone Guide to the Legal Profession 1991   £6.95
- [ ] The Ivanhoe Guide to Chartered Builders 1991   £6.95
- [ ] The Ivanhoe Guide to Chartered Surveyors 1991   £6.95
- [ ] The Ivanhoe Guide to the Engineering Profession 1991   £6.95

Name: . . . .

Address: . . . .

. . . .

. . . . Postcode: . . . .

Please enclose cheque with order, including postage and packing as follows:
1 copy £1; 2 to 5 copies £3 – or take to your local bookshop.

The Ivanhoe Press Limited, Kings Meadow, Ferry Hinksey Road, Oxford
OX2 0DP. Tel: 0865-791006.

Beachcroft Stanleys

Main office: 20 Furnival Street, London EC4A 1BN. Tel: 071-242 1011; Telex: 264607 (BEALAW G); DX 45 London; Fax: 071-831 6630.
Senior partner: Andrew D Kennedy.
Number of partners: 32
Total fee earners: 110
Number of other staff: 230
Firm history: The firm's origins extend back to 1762 in London with strong historical connections also with Bristol and Liverpool. The firm in its present form dates from 1988 with the amalgamation of Beachcrofts and Stanleys & Simpson North.
Firm structure: The firm is organized into four departments representing the major divisions of work undertaken: business, litigation, private client and property. A partner ensures the properly coordinated use of the firm's specialist services to meet the needs of a client. The business of the firm is run by a professional management team which leaves partners with their hands free to make the most active contribution to clients.
Range of client services: Beachcroft Stanleys is a medium sized City of London practice providing comprehensive legal service for a wide range of clients both from the United Kingdom and, increasingly, from overseas. Our clients extend from the family company to the publicly listed company; from the world of advertising to the world of accountants and surveyors; from banks and insurance companies to charitable institutions and bodies; from computer technology to property development and management; from water companies to health authorities and educational bodies. The firm also has many private clients, many of whom are connected in some way with the firm's commercial practice.
Number of trainee solicitors required for 1993: 10
Starting salary: £15,500 (September 1990).
Minimum academic requirements: At least a good second class honours degree (we are happy to consider non-law graduates) but we also place much store on a wider record of activity and experience.
Professional development policies and programmes: A trainee solicitor's programme of training involves spending time in at least three of the departments but, where practicable, with experience in all four. Progress through articles of training is monitored on an individual basis by the firm's Director of Training and a programme of personal development is mapped out for each trainee solicitor. This programme continues where the trainee solicitor continues as an assistant solicitor with the firm. Internal courses and seminar programmes are arranged and, where appropriate, attendance at outside conferences is provided for.
For brochure and application form contact: Dafydd Evans (Director of Training).

Berwin Leighton

Main office: Adelaide House, London Bridge, London EC4R 9HA. Tel: 071-623 3144; Telex: 886420; Fax: 071-623 4416.
Other offices: 135 East 57th Street, New York NY10022. Tel: (0101 212) 754 5400; Fax: (0101 212) 754 5401. The firm has created an extensive network of links with firms both in the EC and internationally.
Chairman: Malcolm Brummer.
Principal executive: Conagh Harpur.
Number of partners: 52
Number of staff: 401 (including partners).
Firm history and structure: Berwin Leighton was formed in 1970 as a result of the merger of two smaller firms. Since then it has grown rapidly and is now a well respected medium sized City firm. It has recently undergone considerable managerial reorganization both at fee-earner level in the setting up of a formal departmental structure and at the business management level through the creation of a Board and the appointment of a comprehensive management support team.
Range of client services: We offer the full complement of legal, technical and commercial advice required by a wide range of corporate clients. We are market leaders in the field of property development with a special reputation in planning and secured lending. Increasingly we are acknowledged for our work in civil litigation, banking and European Community commercial law. We also provide expert advice in the areas of corporate finance, insurance and re-insurance, shipping and aviation.
Number of trainees required for 1993: 15
Minimum academic requirements: 2.2. Non-law graduates considered.
Starting salary: £16,500 (September 1990).
Annual leave entitlement: 22 days.
Professional development policies and programmes: Trainees spend eight months in each of the three major departments – corporate, property and litigation – although there is some room for gaining experience in other areas of work. We have a full education programme running parallel with the practical training. There is a comprehensive range of departmental seminars and the firm recently introduced a structured programme of skills training for assistants. These in-house courses all carry points towards complying with the Law Society's compulsory continuing education regulations and are managed by our Director of Education and Training.
For brochure and application form contact: Hugh Homan.

S J Berwin & Co

Main office: 236 Grays Inn Road, London WC1X 8HB. Tel: 071-278 0444; Telex: 8814928 WINLAW G; Fax: 071-833 2860.
Other offices: Brussels; Prague
Senior partner: C Haan.
Number of partners: 45
Number of staff: 310
Firm history: The firm was founded in 1982 by Stanley Berwin, a former senior director of N M Rothschild & Sons, and has expanded at a remarkable rate achieved by recruiting leading lawyers with a wide range of specialist disciplines. The firm's aim is to provide speedy and positive legal advice that is both commercial and practical, and regards a creative approach as essential.
Range of client services: The firm provides a full range of legal services to financial, industrial and commercial clients, both national and international, as well as advising private clients on trusts, tax planning and asset protection.

There are five main departments (corporate finance, commercial, litigation, property and tax) with expert teams working in particular areas. Although the firm is renowned for handling complex corporate transactions, it also specializes in EEC and competition law, intellectual property, banking, commercial property, planning, media and entertainment law.
Number of trainee solicitors required for 1993: 17-20
Minimum academic requirements: Candidates must be of at least 2:1 ability but need not have read law.
Starting salary: £17,000 (September 1990).
Number of qualified solicitors required for 1991: In addition to trainee solicitors qualifying with the firm, qualified solicitor recruitment will be dictated by client demand.
Starting salary: £27,000 for newly qualified.
Annual leave entitlement: 20 days per annum.
Professional development policies and programmes: Education and training is led by our Director of Professional Development who, with the support of his team, brings together the expertise of partners, leading academics and other specialists to provide courses carefully integrated into the work of the practice and timed to coincide with the individual's career development.
For brochure and application form contact: Michael Trask.

We think this describes us. If this describes you, we would
like to meet you.

In just 8 years S J Berwin & Co has established itself as
a major City firm with a truly international outlook. We
believe this has been achieved through our ability to attract
bright young lawyers with drive, creativity and commitment
who wish to participate in the firm's success.

We expect our articled clerks to share responsibility for
clients' affairs from the very start of their articles. As a
result, the partners take a direct interest in the training
received by our select team of articled clerks.

If you would like to know more about a career with
S J Berwin & Co, write to our Recruitment Partner,
Michael Trask.

S J Berwin & Co

236 Grays Inn Road
London WC1X 8HB

London - Brussels

Biddle & Co

Main office: 1 Gresham Street, London EC2V 7BU. Tel: 071-606 9301 or 071-646 9666 (Mercury); Fax: 071-606 3305.
Senior partner: Robert S Fawssett.
Number of partners: 22
Number of staff: 70
Firm history: First established in the City of London in 1831. Most of the firm's clients were in the textile trades until the Second World War. When that industry moved to the Far East we transferred from rags to riches diversifying into the legal services required by company, commercial, media litigation and pension sectors. We have also retained a thriving private client base.
Range of client services: The largest department deals with company and commercial matters and undertakes work in all areas of corporate law. The firm also has strong litigation, property, tax and private client departments and is particularly well known for its work in the fields of pensions law and media law. Clients include major public companies, property developers, publishing houses, news agencies, newspapers, television companies and private individuals.
Number of trainee solicitors required for 1993: 4
Minimum academic requirements: A minimum 2.2 degree is required. The firm likes its trainee solicitors to be good communicators with cheerful outgoing personalities and is interested in applicants who have achieved in areas outside the law.
Starting salary: £16,000 (September 1990).
Annual leave entitlement: 20 days plus bank holidays.
Professional development policies and programmes: Biddle & Co prides itself on its friendly working environment. A trainee solicitor will gain experience by sitting with partners in four of the firm's departments. In making an offer of articles we are looking not only at the two year training period but also at the individual's potential as a solicitor to join one of our working groups on qualification and progress to eventual partnership.
For brochure and application form contact: Hugh Arthur.

Boodle Hatfield

Main office: 43 Brook Street, London W1Y 2BL. Tel: 071-629 7411; Telex: 261414; Fax: 071-629 2621, DX 53.
Other offices: 7 Town Quay, Southampton SO1 0XN. Tel: 0703-332001; Telex: 477239; Fax: 0703-222480, DX 2005. Villanueva 29, 28001 Madrid, Spain. Tel: 577-5502; Telex: 48564; Fax: 431-0413.
Senior partner: Michael Loup.
Number of partners: 36
Number of staff: 210 approximately.
Firm history: We have been established in the West End of London for over 250 years and have developed from a firm specializing in property and personal tax work into a progressive medium sized firm offering a full range of services to corporate, institutional and individual clients. We have a substantial office in Southampton offering the full range of services to local clients. In 1988 we opened an office in Madrid in conjunction with a long established commercial practice.
Range of client services: Our practice covers, both in London and Southampton, all aspects of legal work relating to property, tax, corporate services including a specialist intellectual property group, commercial and general litigation covering matters from international trade arbitration to domestic disputes. The variety of work within the firm is therefore broad and ensures a good general education during articles.
Number of trainee solicitors required for 1993: 10
Minimum academic requirements: 2.1 standard.
Starting salary: £15,500 at September 1990 with review in December.
Number of qualified solicitors required for 1991: 10
Starting salary: Market rate.
Annual leave entitlement: Four weeks.
Professional development policies and programmes: Our Director of Training, Barry Titman, arranges a full range of internal and external courses and seminars to ensure a full and broad training for all trainees and solicitors. During articles we also second certain trainee solicitors to either ICI or Shell International for periods of up to six months. Over one third of the present partners were articled clerks with the firm.
For brochure and application form contact: Paul Pattinson, Boodle Hatfield, 43 Brook Street, London W1Y 2BL.

Cameron Markby Hewitt

Main office: Sceptre Court, 40 Tower Hill, London EC3N 4BB. Tel: 071-702 2345; Fax: 071-702 2303.

Other offices: Bristol, Brussels, Lloyd's Building.

Senior partner: Mr W T C Shelford.

Number of partners: 69

Number of staff: 520

Firm history: The firm results from the mergers of Cameron Markby, Hewitt Woollacott & Chown and Brafman Morris in May 1989 and is committed to continued growth. Major investment has been made in new premises at Sceptre Court, providing an attractive working environment with the latest generation information systems.

Range of client services: The firm acts for a wide range of national and multinational clients including banks, financial institutions, insurance brokers, trading corporations, media companies and professionals. We have a particular reputation in banking, insolvency, capital markets, venture and development capital, entertainment, insurance litigation and commercial property work, and are recognized for our creative problem solving.

Number of trainee solicitors required for 1993: 30-35

Minimum academic requirements: A good honours degree (law or non-law).

Starting salary: £16,000 (at September 1990) with reviews in March and September.

Number of qualified solicitors required for 1991: Although we retain over eighty per cent of our trainees on qualification we welcome applications from qualified solicitors.

Starting salary: £24,500 (at September 1990).

Annual leave entitlement: 20 working days increasing with length of service.

Professional development policies and programmes: After an introductory training programme, our trainee solicitors spend six months in each of four departments gaining comprehensive experience through working closely with their allocated partners. Our overall aim is to provide a supportive but challenging environment, encouraging trainee solicitors to take on early responsibility. This is done through the provision of high quality work; regular reviews of trainees' performance; and their participation in legal and business seminars and skills training from the in-house training programme. Most trainee solicitors stay with the firm after qualification in the department of their choice.

For brochure and application form contact: Christina Graham (qualified solicitors) or Helen Sheppard (trainee solicitors and vacation work).

Clarks

Main office: Great Western House, Station Road, Reading, Berkshire RG1 1SX. Tel: 0734-585321; Telex: 847646 CLARKS G; Fax: 0734-604611.
Senior partner: Hugh J Williams.
Number of partners: 12
Number of staff: Approximately 100
Firm history: Clarks were established in 1913. The firm has grown rapidly in recent years and in the spring of 1989 moved to its present offices, the former Great Western Hotel, opposite Reading station. Further growth of the firm is planned and the new offices provide ample accommodation to enable this.
Range of client services: Clarks have developed departments to meet the increasingly complex needs of clients. The company department handles a wide range of corporate and financial transactions. There is a substantial property department which deals with all types of commercial and residential property transactions. The commercial/litigation department handles commercial and civil litigation, and also general commercial advisory work and preparation of commercial agreements. The private client department gives a comprehensive service to private clients. Clarks advise and assist on EEC matters and can offer solicitors to deal with matters in French and German.
Number of trainee solicitors required for 1993: 6
Minimum academic requirements: A law degree with at least a good 2.2 or a non-law degree with a 2.1.
Starting salary: Trainee solicitors' starting salary as at September 1990 – £11,000 per annum with increases (of about £1,000) every six months.
Number of qualified solicitors required for 1991: Estimated 6.
Starting salary: The starting salary for newly qualified solicitors as at September 1990 is £19,000 per annum with reviews every six months.
Annual leave entitlement: Four weeks, increasing to five weeks.
Professional development policies and programmes: The firm has a strong programme of in-house training as well as sending staff on courses. In addition to training in legal work, the firm has internal language training programmes for all levels of staff.
For brochure and application form contact: Michael Sippitt.

Clyde & Co

Main office: 51 Eastcheap, London EC3M 1JP. Tel: 071-623 1244; Telex: 884886 CLYDE G; Fax: 071-623 5427, DX 1071 London/City.
Other offices: Guildford, Cardiff, Hong Kong, Sao Paulo, Dubai and Sharjah.
Senior partner: Michael Payton.
Number of partners: 78
Number of staff: 410 (excluding partners).
Firm history, range of client services: Established in 1933, Clyde & Co has expanded rapidly in the last twenty years. The firm has clients in some ninety countries and advises on a wide range of areas of law including international trade, insurance, shipping, company law, property, banking, intellectual property and EC law. In addition to its overseas offices, Clyde & Co has a worldwide network of correspondent lawyers and professional contacts.

The firm provides legal advice to both international and national organizations, including public and private companies and financial institutions.
Number of trainee solicitors required for 1993: 15
Minimum academic requirements: 2.1 degree preferred in any discipline.
Starting salary: £16,000 in September 1990. Salaries reviewed biannually.
Number of qualified solicitors required for 1991: 21
Starting salary: Market rate. Salaries reviewed biannually.
Annual leave entitlement: Four weeks.
Professional development policies and programmes: The emphasis of the firm's training is on giving early responsibility to trainee solicitors and involving them in all aspects of running cases as well as direct contact with clients. This practical 'hands on' experience is complemented by in-house lectures and courses on specialist areas of the law, legal skills, commercial awareness and languages. Our Head of Education and Training arranges an induction course for all trainee solicitors and there are regular in-house training programmes throughout the period of traineeship and after qualification.

Clyde & Co organizes student work placement schemes for law and non-law undergraduates during the summer and Christmas vacations.
For brochure and application form contact: Lisa Wilson, Recruitment Manager, Clyde & Co, 51 Eastcheap, London EC3M 1JP. Alternatively, contact your careers office to see our video or obtain our literature.

Cripps Harries Hall

Principle office: 84 Calverley Road, Tunbridge Wells, Kent TN1 2UP. Tel: 0892-515121; Fax: 0892-515444.
Other offices: Crowborough, Heathfield, Uckfield and Tunbridge Wells (Commercial/FISD).
Senior partner: Duncan Rawson-Mackenzie BA LLB (Cantab) Notary Public.
Managing partner: Jonathan Denny LLB.
Number of partners: 24
Number of staff: 200 (including partners).
Firm history: Cripps Harries Hall was founded in 1852 when William Charles Cripps, later Registrar of the Tunbridge Wells County Court, started in practice. Since then the firm has grown by merger and organically, it is now ranked in the top five in the South East.
Range of client services: The firm has three divisions: *commercial* – covering company, commercial conveyancing and litigation; *private client* – covering domestic litigation, residential and agricultural property, wills, trusts, probate and tax planning; and *finance and investment services* – for both private and business clients covering portfolio management, corporate finance, tax, investment, pensions, insurance and mortgages. (This department is staffed by finance professionals.)
The firm is in the forefront of solicitors offering an integrated finance and investment service to existing and new clients. It has also established associate links with law firms in Paris, Rotterdam, Munich and Madrid.
Management structure: In May 1990, Cripps Harries Hall adopted a formal management structure which includes a full-time Managing Partner; a Partnership Board, composed of the Senior Partner and Heads of Divisions; and devolution of responsibility to heads of departments.
Number of trainee solicitors required for 1993: 6
Minimum academic requirements: Second class honours degree.
Starting salary: Well above Law Society's recommended minimum.
Number of qualified solicitors required for 1991: At least 5.
Annual leave entitlement: Four weeks at start.
Professional development policies and programmes: The firm's director of education coordinates attendance at external courses, lectures and internal departmental seminars to ensure staff are kept up to date with the changes in the law. Trainee solicitors normally spend three of the four six-month training periods in Tunbridge Wells, sharing a room with a partner to whom they usually work directly. It may be possible for French speaking trainee solicitors to spend a short period with a Paris firm of advocats, with whom the firm has an association.
For trainee solicitors brochure and application form contact: Jonathan Denny LLB.

Davies Wallis Foyster

Main office: Harvester House, 37 Peter Street, Manchester M2 5GB. Tel: 061-228 3702; Telex: 668928; Fax: 061-835 2407.
Other offices: 13 Castle Street, Liverpool L2 4XE. Tel: 051-236 6226; Fax: 051-236 3088. 16/17 Richmond Terrace, Blackburn BB1 7BQ. Tel: 0254-678027; Fax: 0254-682146.
Senior partner: James C M Davies.
Number of partners: 42
Number of staff: 220
Firm history: Davies Wallis Foyster is the creation of a merger in November 1989 of a Liverpool firm Davies Wallis, with the Manchester firm Foysters (creating at that time the largest firm based exclusively in the North West). The new firm shows a strong combination of the young dynamic business approach with a traditional professionalism.
Range of client services: The full range of corporate client services are offered including the new construction, planning and personal injury/insurance departments.
Number of trainee solicitors required for 1993: 15
Minimum academic requirements: Preference will be shown to candidates with a 2.1 degree and possibly a second language.
Starting salary: £10,500 (September 1990).
Annual leave entitlement: Four weeks.
Professional development policies and programmes: Davies Wallis Foyster provides a strong training programme for trainee solicitors under the direction of their Director of Training (including induction courses, in-house training and external courses). Such courses include training in languages and personal skills as well as legal technical knowledge.
For brochure and application form contact: Diane B Hughes, Director of Training.

Denton Hall Burgin & Warrens

Main office: Five Chancery Lane, Clifford's Inn, London EC4A 1BU. Tel: 071-242 1212; Telex: 263567 or 262738; Fax: 071-404 0087.
Other UK offices: Milton Keynes.
Overseas offices: Bangkok, Brussels, Hong Kong, Los Angeles, Singapore, Tokyo.
Senior partner: Michael Flint.
Number of partners: 99 (worldwide).
Number of other professional staff: 321 (worldwide).
Number of other staff: 550 (worldwide).
Firm history: Denton Hall Burgin & Warrens can trace its origins back to 1740. The last ten years have been a period of substantial growth and Denton Hall is now one of the largest firms in London and has an extensive international practice. Occupying highly modernized offices the firm has a wide commercial practice and is involved in an extensive range of work worldwide. The profile of the firm is young, with many of the partners in their thirties and forties, and the firm prides itself on its friendly and individual atmosphere.
Firm structure: As a City firm, there is a strong commercial bias. There are four departments (commercial, entertainment, property and litigation) as well as cross-departmental groups such as environmental law and banking. The structure is flexible so that clients' needs can be met. Trainee solicitors are encouraged to gain wide experience during their articles.
Recent major events: Important developments included the opening of offices in Tokyo and Bangkok as part of the firm's commitments overseas. The firm has continued to expand its commercial practice.
Range of client services: The firm places a strong emphasis on corporate and commercial law. It does not practice criminal law or undertake legal aid cases. Areas of particular interest to trainee solicitors are: copyright and entertainment law; energy, oil and gas; flotations; privatization; banking; financial services; mergers and acquisitions; funding; property development; town planning; satellite communications; competition law; construction; and taxation. Cross-departmental groups have been set up specializing in matters such as environmental law, insolvency, banking and the public sector. The firm discourages over-specialization and encourages its lawyers to practise generally within their chosen field, whilst developing areas of expertise.
Number of trainee solicitors required for 1993: Approximately 55.
Minimum academic requirements: Applicants should expect to obtain or should have obtained a good upper second or first. Applications from law or non-law graduates are equally welcome.
Starting salary: £16,700 per annum in September 1990.
Number of qualified solicitors required for 1991: Applications from high-quality candidates are always welcome.

If you'd like to know more about one of the most progressive firms in London, get the whole picture.

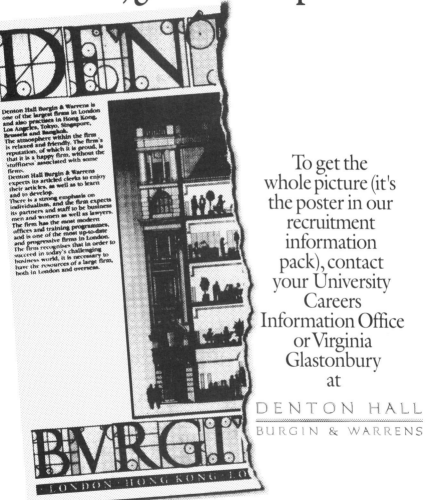

To get the whole picture (it's the poster in our recruitment information pack), contact your University Careers Information Office or Virginia Glastonbury at

DENTON HALL
BURGIN & WARRENS

FIVE CHANCERY LANE · CLIFFORD'S INN · LONDON EC4A 1BU

Starting salary: £25,000 per annum in September 1990.

Annual leave entitlement: 21 days (rising to 26 with service) plus bank holidays.

Professional development policies and programmes: We provide high-quality work experience and a modern programme of training. Our efforts to ensure that our trainee solicitors avoid 'specialization' too early are supplemented by broad training, both legal and non-legal. There is a comprehensive training programme with a wide variety of lectures and subjects. The trainee solicitor will spend six months in three of the departments, sharing an office with a partner or qualified assistant but drawing work from a variety of sources. Early responsibility is given and direct involvement with the client is encouraged. The final six months of articles is spent in an area of work selected after discussion with the trainee solicitor, so far as practicable. Articles are a time of change and growth and the firm supports its trainee solicitors in that change and growth. We encourage our trainee solicitors to develop into independent, commercially minded lawyers. Prospects for employment with the firm after articles are excellent.

For brochure and application form contact: Virginia Glastonbury at Denton Hall Burgin & Warrens. Applications should be sent to Virginia Glastonbury two years ahead of the required starting date for articles and should include a full curriculum vitae and details of two academic referees.

Edge & Ellison

Main office: Rutland House, 148 Edmund Street, Birmingham B3 2JR. Tel: 021-200 2001; Telex: 336370 EDGECO G; Fax: 021-200 1991.
Other offices and links: Brussels, Leicester, Pittsburgh.
Senior partner: J A J Aucott.
Number of partners: 47
Number of staff: 405
Firm history: Founded in 1870, Edge & Ellison is one of the largest firms of commercial lawyers in the UK. Essentially a commercial firm, we act regularly for fifty-nine companies who are publicly quoted on the London Stock Exchange and countless private companies. In addition to our offices in Birmingham and Leicester, we have an office in Brussels and are associated with a firm in Pittsburgh which is represented in nine other cities in the USA as well as Frankfurt, Berlin and Leipzig.
Range of client services: Our corporate finance work includes acquisitions, disposals, mergers and joint ventures. We are particularly active in management buy-outs and flotations. Commercial work covers banking and finance, taxation, EEC law and intellectual property. We also have a special pensions section. Our litigation department handles commercial litigation at all levels, including professional negligence, tribunal and intellectual property work, crime and matrimonial. Building litigation and personal injury are particular areas of expertise.
Number of trainee solicitors required for 1993: 20
Minimum academic requirements: A 2(1) degree is preferred, not necessarily in law.
Starting salary: £12,750 September 1990.
Professional development policies and programmes: We run a structured training programme for both trainee solicitors and qualified staff. We hold informal fortnightly seminars run by partners on a wide range of topics, monthly evening seminars which include outside speakers and experts from within the firm, EEC law seminars, and skills training sessions, including a weekend residential course. Prospects are excellent and many of the present partners served articles with the firm. Overall we are a rapidly expanding, approachable, team-orientated firm, which takes a commercial view of clients' problems. We are proud of our reputation for enjoying our work as well as being good at it.
For brochure and application form contact: Robert Halton, Director of Training and Recruitment.

Eversheds

Eversheds, the first national commercial law firm, has offices in major commercial centres in England and Wales. The firm has 1600 people, including 185 partners, and offers clients the breadth and depth of commercial legal advice normally only associated with a London firm.

Eversheds was created two years ago when six leading regional firms combined and developed a national network and a London practice. Apart from the London office, which practises under the name Eversheds, each of the six firms currently practises under its established name and maintains its leading position in its own region.

Eversheds was created for two prime reasons: to provide clients in the regions and London the increased range of specialist advice which is needed now and increasingly into the 21st century, and to give employees the quality of work, mobility and attention to training which the largest organizations offer.

Offices, numbers of partners and staff:

Member	Locations	Partners	Total Staff
Alexander Tatham	Manchester Warrington London	21	100
Daynes Hill & Perks	Norwich Great Yarmouth London	45	230
Evershed Wells & Hinds	Birmingham Derby, Nottingham London	52	420
Eversheds	London	8	40
Hepworth & Chadwick	Leeds London	23	270
Ingledew Botterell	Middlesbrough, Newcastle London	21	120
Phillips & Buck	Cardiff London	23	90

Range of client services: The firm has established national groups which cover a comprehensive range of commercial legal advice for UK and international clients. The major areas include corporate finance, commercial, intellectual property, property, litigation, insolvency, employment and private client. In addition, groups have been formed covering environmental law, fraud protection and European law as well as industry groups such as brewing, construction, shipping and banking.

Number of trainee solicitors required for 1993: Approximately 100.

Minimum academic requirements: A good second class honours degree, although it need not be in law.

Trainee solicitors: Trainee solicitors can work in the office of their choice, and with Eversheds get the best of both worlds. The increased range of specialist advice that the firm's clients demand means that they get the quantity and quality of training needed to provide this. But they also get the individual attention from being in a smaller sized regional firm.

Professional development policies and programmes: The establishment of a comprehensive, unified training programme throughout Eversheds has been one of the firm's top priorities, and the Director of Training is now responsible for devising training courses for all trainee solicitors, assistant solicitors and partners. Training also takes place through the national specialist groups at regular national conferences. The conference topics cover all the key areas of legal practice.

Eversheds' trainee solicitors gain experience in at least four different departments, under the direct supervision of a partner, and are trained in procedures for both disputed and undisputed cases.

For brochure and application form please write to the location of your choice:

Birmingham: Philip Williams, Evershed Wells & Hind, 10 Newhall Street, Birmingham B3 3LX. Tel: 021-233 2001.

Cardiff: Lynn Challinor, Phillips & Buck, Fitzalan House, Fitzalan Road, Cardiff CF2 1XZ. Tel: 0222-471147.

Leeds: Robert Chapman, Hepworth & Chadwick, Cloth Hall Court, Infirmary Street, Leeds LS1 2JB. Tel: 0532-430391.

London: Richard Winter, 1 Gunpowder Square, Printer Street, London EC4A 3DE. Tel: 071-936 2553.

Manchester: Janet Knowles, Alexander Tatham, 30 St Ann Street, Manchester M2 3DB. Tel: 061-236 4444.

Newcastle: Stephen Mills, Ingledew Botterell, Milburn House, Dean Street, Newcastle upon Tyne NE1 1NP. Tel: 091-261 1661.

Norwich: Chris Gillham, Daynes Hill & Perks, Holland Court, The Close, Norwich NR1 4DX. Tel: 0603-611212.

Nottingham & Derby: Nigel Sternberg, Evershed Wells & Hind, 14 Fletcher Gate, Nottingham NG1 2FX. Tel: 0602-506201.

Foot & Bowden

Main office: 70/76 North Hill, Plymouth, Devon PL4 8HH. Tel: 0752-663416; Telex: 45223; Fax: 0752-671802.
Senior partner: The Lord Foot.
Number of partners: 19
Number of other professional staff: 30
Number of other staff: 85
Firm history: Isaac Foot founded the firm nearly one hundred years ago. Since then the Foot family connection has been maintained with the current senior partner being Lord Foot, who sits on the Liberal Democrat benches in the House of Lords. The partnership is presently nineteen, and enjoys practising law both as colleagues and friends together. The firm has a long tradition of partners being absent for extramural activities, ranging from Isaac Foot's membership of the Asquith government in the twenties through to one of the present partners reaching the Presidency of the Law Society. Another has commanded, for two years, full time, his Territorial Army Regiment, while yet another is very active in local politics.
Range of client services: The firm's aim is to provide a complete service for all clients, both private and commercial. There is a specialist mineral and planning law department led by a senior partner, William Jones. There is a specialist shipping law department specially staffed by solicitors recruited from London, who are experts in both wet and dry marine work. In addition, there is a specialist licensing department led by a senior consultant, W Anthony Daniel.
Number of trainee solicitors required for 1993: 8
Starting salary: Commensurate with other leading firms in the area.
Number of qualified solicitors required for 1991: 6
Starting salary: Commensurate with other leading firms in the area.
Annual leave entitlement: Four weeks.
For brochure and application form contact: Jane S A Lister.

A SOUND FUTURE
IN PLYMOUTH

Plymouth is not only the centre of West Country tourism, it is the major commercial centre. Recently voted the most desirable place to live in the country, it is an excellent city in which to begin a law career.

Plymouth is steeped in history, Foot & Bowden also have a long and illustrious history of their own. The practice will shortly be celebrating its 100th Anniversary.

Beginning your career with Foot & Bowden will mean completing your training in a traditional but progressive firm. Foot & Bowden will make certain your tuition is thorough, enjoyable and will actively promote early contact with clients.

Foot & Bowden offer an excellent starting salary, together with genuine prospects for a sound future.

Get ready for tomorrow by writing to Jane S. A. Lister, Managing Partner, Foot & Bowden, 70-76 North Hill, Plymouth, Devon PL4 8HH.

FOOT & BOWDEN

CONTACT FORM

To: The Head of Recruitment

. . . .

. . . .

. . . .

THE IVANHOE GUIDE TO
THE LEGAL PROFESSION 1991

I have been interested to read about your organization in the above publication
and would be grateful if you would send me a copy of your brochure and an
application form.

Signed . . . .   Date . . . .

*Name . . . .

*Address . . . .

. . . .

. . . .

*Please print

Frere Cholmeley

Main office: 28 Lincoln's Inn Fields, London WC2A 3HH. Tel: 071-405 7878; Fax: 071-405 9056.
Other offices: Berlin, Brussels, Milan, Monte Carlo, Paris.
Chairman: Bruce Brodie.
Chief executive: Tim Razzall.
Number of partners: 50 (143 qualified lawyers including partners).
Number of staff: 391
Firm history: Founded in 1750. Since the 1950s Frere Cholmeley has developed its comprehensive corporate and commercial practice both in the UK and overseas and it is now one of the leading European law firms. The Paris office was opened in 1968, Monte Carlo in 1979, Milan in 1988, and Brussels and Berlin in 1990. Further expansion is planned in Europe.
Range of client services: The *company and commercial department* advises on all aspects of corporate finance and banking, undertaking major transactional work for listed and non-listed clients. The *litigation department* has experience in all areas of commercial litigation and a high proportion of its work has an international element; the Anglo-German group strengthens the international team. Other cross-department groups include aviation, employment, environmental, employment, entertainment and tax. The *property department* has a broad practice in commercial development and planning work, working with major international property organizations. The *private client department* offers an extensive range of services to individual clients.
Number of trainee solicitors required for 1993: 30
Minimum academic requirements: Law and non-law graduates with 2.1 ability.
Starting salary: £16,250
Number of qualified solicitors required for 1991: 25
Starting salary: £25,000 (1990 qualifiers)
Annual leave entitlement: 20 working days plus additional leave at Christmas. Increases with time at firm.
Professional development policies and programmes: The firm has a training officer who is responsible for the continuing education programme. This includes departmental seminars and lectures given by internal and external speakers on a wide range of legal topics. In addition, there are lectures on non-legal topics related to the City and other business subjects. Trainee solicitors also receive practical and management development training.
For brochure and application form contact: Paul Roberts. A brochure and audio tape are available to inform applicants about articles at Frere Cholmeley.

Freshfields

Main office: Whitefriars, 65 Fleet Street, London EC4Y 1HS. Tel: 071-936 4000; Telex: 889292; Fax: 071-832 7001.
Other offices: Brussels, Frankfurt, Hong Kong, New York, Paris, Singapore, Tokyo.
Senior partner: J K Grieves.
Number of partners: 98 worldwide.
Number of staff: 1014
Firm history and structure: Established in the 1700s as advisers to the Bank of England, Freshfields has always been highly regarded among the leading City firms. It is evolving into a major European player as part of the overall global strategy.

The London office, housed in new premises on Fleet Street, is divided into four departments: company, litigation, real property, and tax.
Range of client services: The main emphasis of the work is service to corporate clients and financial institutions. The firm provides comprehensive legal services of exceptional quality worldwide.

The practice is well balanced and includes a number of specialized practice areas. Lawyers are given a broad training before they begin to specialize, and are therefore able to solve complex problems from a wide knowledge base. The information and technological support available to lawyers is exceptional.
Number of trainee solicitors required for 1993: 70-80
Minimum academic requirements: Candidates must be of 2.1 calibre. Applications from non-law graduates are welcomed.
Starting salary: £16,550 for new trainees, rising to £26,000 for newly qualified solicitors, September 1990.
Annual leave entitlement: 20 days.
Professional development: Freshfields has a leading reputation for the quality of the training and career development.

Trainee solicitors undertake a range of technical and skills courses which supplement experience of practical work. Trainees are given considerable responsibility and frequently meet clients on transactions.
For brochure and application form contact: Mr G A Whalley at the above address.

THE REWARDS OF SERVING YOUR ARTICLES AT FRESHFIELDS TRANSCEND THE MERELY FINANCIAL

Exotic pleasures well outside the law await the articled clerk at Freshfields. From the sublimities of seven-a-side rugby to the hurly-burly of Brahms at the Barbican Centre (tickets at subsidised prices) a myriad of cultural and sporting delights await you.

At frequent intervals in this round of pleasure your professional competence and career prospects will be polished to a lustre with one of the City of London's leading international law firms. You will explore the challenges and rewards to be found in Freshfields' Company and Commercial, Litigation, Real Property, Tax and Private Client Departments. You may also be asked to work in one of our offices abroad.

It is recognised that to serve Articles at Freshfields is to graduate with honours in a highly professional school from where, either within Freshfields or on other horizons, every prospect gleams.

Our 1991 brochure will be with your Careers Advisory Service from April. For a personal copy of this programme of the pleasures, as well as the rewards, of serving articles at Freshfields, please write to or phone Guy Whalley, Freshfields, Whitefriars, 65 Fleet Street, London EC4Y 1HT. Telephone: 071-936 4000.

FRESHFIELDS
LONDON · BRUSSELS · PARIS
NEW YORK · HONG KONG · SINGAPORE · TOKYO

Herbert Smith

Main office: Exchange House, Primrose Street, London EC2A 2HS. Tel: 071-374 8000; Fax: 071-496 0067.

Overseas offices: Brussels, Hong Kong, New York and Paris.

Overseas links: Links with lawyers throughout the world.

Senior partner: John Rowson.

Number of partners: 84

Number of staff: 1000

Firm history: Herbert Smith was founded in 1882 by Norman Herbert Smith. It has grown particularly rapidly in recent years and we moved to new offices in London in 1990. Our growth is the result of the effort of all those working at Herbert Smith and not the result of a merger with another firm.

Firm structure: Herbert Smith is organized into groups in order to give a top level of service to clients in all aspects of commercial work, much of it international. The groups are flexible particularly in areas involving different areas such as environmental and insolvency matters.

An example of our commitment to the future is the development of our own information database to which each fee earner (including each trainee solicitor) has access from the computer terminal and screen on his or her desk.

Trainee solicitors are given experience in a wide range of the firm's work.

Range of client services: Herbert Smith provides a full range of services to cover all aspects of UK and international commercial work.

Number of trainee solicitors required for 1993: At least 75.

Minimum academic requirements: Herbert Smith welcomes applications from those with non-law degrees as well as those who are studying law. Candidates will need to be bright and able to get on with things. They will also be people who will be able to understand and deal with clients and be able to take responsibility.

Starting salary: Herbert Smith provides an excellent renumeration package (including bursaries during years spent studying for the Law Society exams).

Opportunities for qualified solicitors: We are always looking for bright people who are anxious to get involved in top quality work.

Annual leave entitlement: 22 days per year.

Training: Training and information are vital at all stages of a legal career. In addition to the practical experience of working on top quality matters, Herbert Smith provides a full range of in-house training programmes for both trainee solicitors and qualified lawyers.

For brochure and application form contact: Stephen Barnard.

Lewis Silkin

Main office: 1 Butler Place, Buckingham Gate, London SW1H 0PT. Tel: 071-222 8191; Telex: 269677; Fax: 071-222 4633.

Overseas offices and links: Lewis Silkin does not have any overseas offices but enjoys very close links with lawyers in many other jurisdictions, especially the USA, France, Israel, Switzerland, Australia, Italy and Spain.

Senior partner: John Fraser MP.

Number of partners: 19

Number of other professional staff: 41

Number of other staff: Approximately 100 (total, including partners).

Firm history: Lewis Silkin has its roots in the 1920s but the parliamentary and ministerial careers of Lewis, father of John and Sam and of the first Town and County Planning Act, delayed the real growth of the practice until the 1950s. Now the firm has expanded to a point at which it can offer its clients a range of experience from representation before the local magistrates to a comprehensive legal service for the company going public.

Firm structure: Administratively the firm is run by a lead partner, who reports to a management board. Clientwise, the office is divided into corporate, property and litigation departments. The firm has an association with Glazer Delmar a high street practice in Peckham, London SE15 which allows trainees the opportunity of spending six months doing high street work.

Major events in the past year: The firm has continued its controlled growth responding to the increasing demands of the firm's successful clients and has aimed to provide a 'one-stop' legal service of a consistently high quality. Lewis Silkin has continued its pattern of innovative marketing to reflect the personal style of service it provides. The firm has been appointed as the sole UK representative of the European Advertising Lawyers Association.

Range of client services: There is a variety in our practice and client base which is possibly unique. Many of our fee earners are experienced in particular areas, but we do not have hermetically sealed compartments as we do not believe that in so doing we can best service our clients. For the 'pigeon hole' conscious, however, our corporate work includes acquisitions, mergers, flotations, management buy-outs, start-ups, BES work, competition and anti-trust, taxation planning, trust and probate, commercial contracts and licensing. Within the property sector the range and depth of the work continues with commercial property transactions, planning, housing association work, institutional and domestic mortgaging, estate acquisition and disposal. Litigation and pre-litigation advice covers heavy commercial, building and construction, insolvency, intellectual property, immigration, crime (including white collar and all aspects of regulatory work) and personal injury.

Number of trainee solicitors required for 1993: 6 (recruited for 1992: 12)
Minimum academic requirements: Minimum 2.2 law or other degree.
Starting salary: £13,500 (September 1990).
Number of qualified solicitors required for 1991: 3
Starting salary: Market rate,
Annual leave entitlement: Four weeks.
Professional development policies and programmes: Each department has a training budget which funds both internal and external courses on legal and management issues. All professional staff are appraised every six months reflecting Lewis Silkin's commitment to training and assessment.
For brochure and application form contact: Andrew Thomas, Trainee Solicitor Recruitment Partner, 1 Butler Place, Buckingham Gate, London SW1H OPT.

Lovell White Durrant

Main office: 65 Holborn Viaduct, London EC1A 2DY. Tel: 071-236 0066; Telex: 887122 LWD G/919014 LWD G; Fax: 071-248 4212/071-236 0084.
Other offices and links: London, New York, Brussels, Paris, Tokyo, Hong Kong, Beijing.
Senior partner: Peter N Gerrard until 31st April 1991; Cavan Taylor from 1st May 1991.
Number of partners: 119
Number of staff: 1154
Range of client services: The firm provides a full range of services to the business client. The principal areas of advice are: banking; commercial and private company; computers and telecommunications; construction and engineering; corporate finance; corporate tax; EEC and competition law; employment, industrial relations and pensions; energy; environmental law; financial services; insolvency; insurance and reinsurance; intellectual property; international trade; investigations and enquiries; investment funds, litigation and arbitration; media law; planning and rating; private client and tax planning; product liability; property; shipping; venture capital and management buy-outs.
Number of trainee solicitors required for 1993: 80
Starting salary: From 1st September 1990 – £16,250 (next review 1st March 1991).
Annual leave entitlement: 22 days per year.
For brochure and application form contact: Mrs Lynda Neal, Lovell White Durrant, 65 Holborn Viaduct, London EC1A 2DY. Tel: 071-236 0066.

International Practice at large

We are one of the very largest City firms, with offices in London, New York, Brussels, Paris, Hong Kong and Tokyo. Our clients come to us for advice on all aspects of commercial law – much of it with an international element. EEC and competition law have long been important parts of our practice and our Brussels office was established in 1972.

We aim to provide our trainee solicitors with a broad range of practical experience without over-specialisation, and have also developed a full programme of seminars and talks to supplement practical training. We carefully monitor career progress, but that is not inconsistent with giving early responsibility.

There are good opportunities to travel and to live abroad, both during training and on qualification.

We expect hard work and commitment, but the rewards are good and the atmosphere in our offices is friendly and informal. There is a busy agenda of social and sporting activities.

While the majority of those who join us have law degrees, we encourage applicants from other disciplines and are especially interested in science and modern language graduates.

For further information about training and vacation work please
contact:-
Mrs Lynda Neal,
Lovell White Durrant,
65 Holborn Viaduct,
London EC1A 2DY.

LONDON · NEW YORK · BRUSSELS · PARIS · HONG KONG · TOKYO · BEIJING

Macfarlanes

Main office: 10 Norwich Street, London EC4A 1BD. Tel: 071-831 9222; Fax: 071-831 9607.
Senior partner: Vanni E Treves.
Number of partners: 38
Number of staff: 364
Firm history, structure and recent major events: Founded in 1875, Macfarlanes is a medium-sized City firm which has grown rapidly in the last twenty years. The firm has four main departments – corporate, commercial and banking; property; litigation; and tax and financial planning. Many of the firm's clients are based overseas and the firm has close professional and personal links with leading lawyers worldwide. It has recently opened a Brussels office with O'Melveny & Myers – one of the leading law firms in the US – and Siméon & Associés – a distinguished French firm.
Range of client services: Macfarlanes has a broad international practice representing substantial corporate and institutional clients. The *corporate, commercial and banking department* has particular expertise in SE and USM, venture capital, fund and management buy-out work. Its banking sector advises UK and overseas banks. The *litigation department* specializes in international and Privy Council work. The *property department* represents major national and international institutional and development clients and advises on planning and environmental issues. The *tax and financial planning department* offers sophisticated tax advice to families and individuals both in the UK and abroad.
Number of trainee solicitors required for 1993: 25 (**recruited for 1992:** 25)
Minimum academic requirements: 2.1 degree.
Starting salary: £15,500 per annum (September 1990).
Number of qualified solicitors required for 1991: 25
Starting salary: £24,500 per annum (September 1990).
Annual leave entitlement: Initially 20 working days.
Professional development policies and programmes: The firm's Director of Training organizes an extensive continuing education programme recognized by the Law Society. Trainee solicitors usually spend six months in each department which ensures widely based articles. Solicitors are regularly seconded abroad. Thirty out of the thirty-eight partners were articled with the firm.
For brochure and application form contact: Mrs Tricia Brett.

MACFARLANES

Nabarro Nathanson

Main office: 50 Stratton Street, London W1X 5FL. Tel: 071-493 9933; Fax: 071-629 7900 Dx No: 77.

Regional office: Doncaster.

Senior partner: Jeffrey Greenwood.

Number of partners: 96

Number of staff: 800

Firm history: Nabarro Nathanson was formed in 1958 from the merger of two older established Piccadilly firms, whose origins date back to the beginning of this century. Our present offices in Stratton Street, near St James, are conveniently central for clients in the City and Central London, and for the convenience of our clients in the North of England we have a regional office in Doncaster, South Yorkshire. We have grown dramatically over the years in order to meet the continuing growth in demand of our services.

Range of client services: The majority of our work is in the commercial field; our clients range from one-man companies to multinationals and governments. We have specialist departments handling a wide range of commercial work: corporate, property, litigation, tax and trusts, pensions, construction, public sector and planning. We also have teams working in banking and finance, EEC and environmental, share incentives, insolvency and intellectual property. International work is undertaken by the majority of these departments.

Number of trainee solicitors required for 1993: 30 in London, 8 in Doncaster.

Minimum academic requirements: Applicants must be of 2.1 ability, not necessarily with a degree in law.

Starting salary: London: £16,500 (September 1990) rising in stages to £18,750 in the last six months of articles; Doncaster: £12,500 (September 1990) rising in stages to £14,750 in the last six months of articles. These figures are reviewed every six months to maintain competitiveness.

Annual leave entitlement: 21 working days plus extra as service lengthens.

Professional development policies and programmes: Our trainee solicitors are involved in a comprehensive training programme organized by the Director of Legal Education. We have made legal, business and personal skills a major priority and are well known for our coherent and integrated training strategy which is complemented by our dedicated training centre. There are opportunities to work overseas and we have an active programme to develop associations worldwide.

For trainee solicitors brochure and application form contact: Ms Pat Haynes, Head of Legal Personnel.

A PARTICULAR KIND OF TRAINEE SOLICITOR

The type of law firm you choose depends entirely on the type of person you are. You are intelligent, have a lively inquiring mind, and like hard work. You sense that you would give your best in a professional but informal and relaxed atmosphere.

You are considering the law, but feel that your outgoing personality may not be compatible with what you perceive law firms to be.

If we have described you here, we have also described a Nabarro Nathanson person – we have already attracted some of the brightest, most original minds.

We are one of the UK's leading law practices with offices in London and Doncaster, South Yorkshire. We have seven departments offering scope for a tremendous career. We are highly professional and successful. We have doubled in size in the past five years to meet the continuing growth in demand for our services.

We are a young firm (our partners are, on average, under 45) with fresh ideas and we are looking for people to take us into a bright future.

Our refreshing approach demands the highest professional standards, the pursuit of excellence and a lot of hard work. However, individual efforts are recognised and well-rewarded. We encourage our trainees to take on as much responsibility as their talents and experience will allow.

If you like what you have read so far, come and see for yourself how different we are, meet our partners and talk to our trainee solicitors. What they have to tell you could convince you that we are just your type.

We offer top salaries and are interested in high calibre graduates (not necessarily with a degree in law).

Telephone or write to: Pat Haynes, Head of Legal Personnel

REGULATED IN THE CONDUCT OF INVESTMENT BUSINESS BY THE LAW SOCIETY.   A Particular Kind of Law Firm

CONTACT FORM

To: The Head of Recruitment

. . . .

. . . .

. . . .

THE IVANHOE GUIDE TO
THE LEGAL PROFESSION 1991

I have been interested to read about your organization in the above publication and would be grateful if you would send me a copy of your brochure and an application form.

Signed . . . .   Date . . . .

*Name . . . .

*Address . . . .

. . . .

. . . .

*Please print

Slater Heelis

Main office: 71 Princess Street, Manchester M2 4HL. Tel: 061-228 3781; Telex: 669568 Maxim G; Fax: 061-236 5282.
Other offices: Sale.
Senior partner: R J Groarke.
Number of partners: 17
Number of staff: 125
Firm history: Slater Heelis was founded in 1773 in Manchester. An office in Sale was opened after World War One. The firm is one of the leading practices in the North West having been involved in the commercial activity of the region for over 200 years.
Range of client services: Slater Heelis conducts an extensive commercial practice in the North West and nationally on a broad client base. Its clients include banks and other financial institutions, listed USM and private companies in industrial and property sectors including UK subsidiaries of multinationals. The firm is particularly well known for banking, corporate work (including Stock Exchange), commercial property, commercial litigation, insolvency and employment law.
Number of trainee solicitors required for 1993: 7
Minimum academic requirements: The firm seeks to attract applicants of high academic ability but gives equal consideration to personal qualities.
Starting salary: Comparable with leading provincial firms.
Number of qualified solicitors required for 1991: 4
Annual leave entitlement: 20 days plus bank holidays.
Professional development policies and programmes: Slater Heelis seeks to provide good training for its staff and the highest possible service for its clients by maintaining a strong all round team which handles complex and high grade work within a friendly but highly professional atmosphere.
For brochure and application form contact: Christopher Dunn.

Slaughter and May

Main office: 35 Basinghall Street, London EC2V 5DB. Tel: 071-600 1200; Telex: 883486/888926; Fax: 071-726 0038/071-600 0289.
Other offices: Paris, Hong Kong, New York, Tokyo, Brussels.
Senior partner: G B Inglis.
Number of partners: 92 worldwide.
Number of staff: 1,250 worldwide.
Firm history: The firm celebrated its centenary in 1989; its founders William Slaughter and William May quickly established a thriving practice in the City, the demand for their services resulting from the combination of excellence in legal technique and practical common sense. That tradition has been followed ever since, both in the UK and overseas, new demands being met by new skills and services. The international work has been a feature from the start.
Range of client services: The great majority of our work is in the commercial field; our clients range from one-man companies to multinationals and governments. We meet all their needs in commercial law except admiralty. Complementing the firm's main activities in the corporate and financial field are the vital specialist departments including litigation/arbitration, property, tax, pensions/employment, EC/competition, financial services and intellectual property. We can put a team together on any transaction because of this breadth of expertise (and our services are available throughout the world).
Number of trainee solicitors required for 1993: 75
Minimum academic requirements: Candidates must be of 2.1 ability but do not need to have read law.
Starting salary: £16,600 (November 1990) rising in stages to £19,900 in the last six months of articles. On qualifying, £26,000.
Annual leave entitlement: 22 working days.
Professional development policies and programmes: It is the firm's policy to meet all challenges and changes through forward planning, good training (carried out principally by our own professional training staff) and new specialist skills where necessary. We aim to maintain an outstanding team of people who enjoy working together. Even though we are one of the largest firms, quality is more important than quantity; size alone is not enough.
Applications and enquiries should be made in writing to: Neil Morgan, Head of Personnel.

The partners of Slaughter and May invite you to an informal cocktail party on 7th September 1993 at 6.00pm to mark the start of your articles.

Even on your first day
you will be staying late.

After signing your Articles with ̩ughter and May you will need to ̩k hard to succeed.

However, you will find we ̩k just as hard at ensuring your ̩rts are rewarded.

Our success has been based on ̩ing individuals an environment ̩ch allows their different talents to ̩elop and also recognises their ̩evements.

That way we know they will

give their best. It is also the way we have come to advise some of the world's biggest companies.

Our selection process is individual in its approach.

We welcome graduates of at least 2.1 standard from any discipline, not just Law. If you have the person-

ality, intellect and common sense to be 'part of the team', then you are probably right for Slaughter and May.

For more details on how to apply for articles, please write to Neil Morgan, Head of Personnel, Slaughter and May, 35 Basinghall Street, London EC2V 5DB.

SLAUGHTER AND MAY

LONDON · PARIS · HONG KONG · NEW YORK · TOKYO · BRUSSELS

N INTERNATIONAL FIRM WITH AN INDIVIDUAL APPROACH.

Titmuss Sainer & Webb

Main office: 2 Serjeants' Inn, London EC4Y 1LT. Tel: 071-583 5353; Telex: 23823 ADVICE G; Fax: 071-353 3683/2830 DX 30 London.
Managing partner: Dick Russell.
Senior partner: Michael Smith.
Number of partners: 49
Number of staff: 330
Firm history, range of client services: Titmuss Sainer & Webb is one of the City's leading medium-sized commercial firms, highly regarded for the quality of its work, innovative training and friendly working environment. The firm is organized into corporate, property and litigation departments and specialist multidisciplinary teams handling commercial, banking, insolvency, employment, taxation, construction and planning and rating law. Our clients include UK and overseas based listed and private companies from a wide cross section of industry and commerce. We are committed to further well-planned growth and to the constant development of our resources, skills and training initiatives to build upon our very favourable position in the market for legal services.
Number of trainee solicitors required for 1993: 20-25
Minimum academic requirements: Second-class degree.
Starting salary: £16,500 (September 1990).
Professional development policies and programmes: Trainee solicitors are given every opportunity to gain a broad knowledge of commercial law. Recruitment is limited in order to give the fullest attention to training and career development and allow direct client contact and responsibility at an early stage. Articles are divided into six four-monthly periods; eight months in a department is often split into four months' general work followed by four months' specialization in a unit of the trainee's choice. Training is essentially practical but seminars and courses, including instruction in management matters, are organized and coordinated throughout articles by our full-time Director of Training, Professor John Adams.

Titmuss Sainer & Webb is at a particularly exciting stage in its development. It is large enough to offer full team support and sophisticated back up and administration – small enough to allow trainee solicitors to make their mark and play a significant role in its future: a firm which we hope they, like the majority of our past trainees, will enjoy remaining with after qualification. The firm also offers a limited number of final-year students an opportunity to join the summer vacation visit scheme.
For brochure and application form contact: Nick Beattie.

Turner Kenneth Brown

Main office: 100 Fetter Lane, London EC4A 1DD. Tel: 071-242 6006; Fax: 071-242 3003.

Other UK offices: Abbot's House, Abbey Street, Reading RG1 3BD. Tel: 0734-504700; Fax: 0734-505640.

Overseas offices and links: Brussels, Dubai (associate) Hong Kong.

Senior partner: David R Wightman.

Number of partners: 66

Number of other professional staff: 153

Number of other staff: 245

Firm history: Although it can trace its history back over 200 years the firm is very forward looking.

In 1983, the twenty-nine partners in the law firms Kenneth Brown Baker Baker and Turner Peacock merged to form Turner Kenneth Brown. That merger was closely followed by a move to 100 Fetter Lane. Since then the firm has also opened offices in Hong Kong, Brussels and in the M4 Corridor at Reading.

The further merger in May 1989 with the long established City firm of Lawrence Messer & Co, heralded another stage in its development as a major City firm.

Firm structure: The firm has the following main departments: company/commercial, property, litigation, private client, taxation and intellectual property/information technology. In addition there are a number of less formal groups dealing either with specific areas of law (eg employment and immigration) or with particular types of client (eg engineering and construction, the public sector).

Major events in the past year: 1990 was yet another eventful year for TKB. In October 1990 the firm announced a formal alliance with Thelen, Marrin, Johnson and Bridges of the United States. The alliance combines the capabilities of TKB's 219 lawyers in four offices with Thelen's 350 lawyers in the US and Hong Kong and is the latest step towards its goal of becoming a truly multinational firm.

Range of client services:

- *Commercial property* – TKB has one of the largest commercial property departments in the UK and covers the whole range of property transactions.

- *Corporate finance* – TKB advises on stock exchange requirements and the raising of equity or debt in all its various manifestations.

- *Mergers, acquisitions and disposals* – TKB has experience in a variety of public and private company transactions both large and small.

- *Management buy-outs* – TKB advises on all types and scales of MBO and its experience also covers business expansion schemes and venture capital investment schemes.

- *International and national dispute resolution* – in addition to its long experience in all forms of traditional litigation and arbitration, TKB is in the forefront of developing and implementing other forms of commercial dispute resolution.

- *Information technology/intellectual property* – clients include both users and major suppliers of computer hardware and software and the firm has a dedicated department handling this area of work. As well as advising on IT contracts it also provides guidance on protection of intellectual property rights, including advice on the new Copyright, Designs and Patents Act.

- Other areas in which TKB has considerable experience include: banking, competition, construction, European and competition law, employment/ immigration, financial services, licensing, planning property services, private client, tax.

Number of trainee solicitors required for 1993: Approximately 35.

Minimum academic requirements: 2.2 degree (not necessarily in law).

Starting salary: £17,000 (September 1990).

Number of qualified solicitors required for 1991: No upper or lower limit but probably around 30 (including qualifying trainee solicitors).

Starting salary: Negotiable.

Annual leave entitlement: Four weeks (plus extra day at Christmas and Easter).

Professional development policies and programmes: Peter Willoughby, former Professor of Law at Hong Kong University, is TKB's full-time Training Partner and he has established an extensive training and development programme for trainee solicitors, assistant solicitors and partners (see article on 'Training with a large firm' in this publication).

Considerable resources are devoted to trainee solicitors training and ensuring that qualified solicitors continue to develop expertise and knowledge in their particular fields. This is achieved by a combination of in-house training, Law Society and other external training courses.

For brochure and application form contact: Personnel Manager, Turner Kenneth Brown, 100 Fetter Lane, London EC4A 1DD.

FLAKEY DULL & BORRING

INVITE YOU TO

JOIN US AS AN ARTICLED CLERK

AND EVENTUALLY DIE.

WHAT FLAKEY DULL & BORRING ARE LOOKING FOR IS A YOUNG LAD OR SIMILAR WHO KNOWS ITS PLACE, AND APPRECIATES THAT ITS PLACE WILL BE IN THE KITCHEN MAKING TEA, OR AT THE COPYING MACHINE MAKING COPIES.

THE PRACTICE OF THE LAW HAS AFTER ALL LONG BEEN SUFFICIENTLY COMPETITIVE; WE AT FLAKEY DULL & BORRING SEE NO FUTURE IN ENCOURAGING YOUNG INTERLOPERS TO ACHIEVE SUCH COMPETENCE THAT THEY ONE DAY VIE WITH US FOR CLIENTS.

THE PREFERRED CANDIDATE'S FATHER WILL HAVE A TROUT FARM IN ONE OF THE MORE SALUBRIOUSLY-EQUIPPED GLENS OF THAT REGION OF EMPIRE TO THE NORTH OF THE BORDER, AND BE PREPARED TO ENTRUST ALL FUTURE LEGAL MATTERS TO THIS FIRM.

THE CANDIDATE ITSELF WILL BE APPRECIATIVE OF THE RICH VEIN OF TRADITION IN WHICH THE FIRM OF FLAKEY DULL AND BORRING HAS ST... SINCE ITS ESTABLISHMENT IN DICKENSIAN...

Before you tear off and join the wrong law firm, talk to Turner Kenneth Brown.

TKB is one of Britain's biggest law firms, with offices in London, Brussels, Hong Kong, and a solid alliance with a major American practice.

Your training will be of the highest standard because you'll work at the highest level.

You'll be part of a senior partner or experienced assistant's team for every one of the four six-month seats which make up your articles.

At TKB you'll polish existing skills and develop new ones by the simple process of being part of the action.

Might we suggest you tear off and use the address details listed below?

TURNER KENNETH BROWN

Applications to: The Personnel Manager, Turner Kenneth Brown, 100 Fetter Lane, London EC4A 1DD.

Watson, Farley & Williams

Main office: Minories House, 2-5 Minories, London EC3N 1BJ. Tel: 071-481 1000; Telex: 8955707; Fax: 071-488 1586.
Overseas offices: Athens, New York, Oslo, Paris.
Senior partner: Alastair Farley.
Number of partners: 29
Number of staff: 224
Firm history: Established in 1982, the firm has moved quickly to develop an international commercial practice.
Firm structure: There is a continuous need for multidisciplinary advice so lawyers, although organized into divisions, are encouraged to work as multidisciplinary teams.
Recent major events: The affiliated office in New York opened in 1990 to practise English and New York law, and broke new ground by achieving an international partnership of lawyers in different jurisdictions.
Range of client services: The firm conducts an extensive commercial practice developed from its core specialization, shipping. With a client base of ship owners, aircraft companies, oil and gas corporations, banks and financial institutions, it has a worldwide clientele. The firm's areas of expertise include shipping, banking, asset and project financing, taxation, commercial property, company, EEC and insolvency law and commercial litigation. Controlled overseas expansion enables the partnership to continue the tradition of personal service upon which the firm is founded.
Number of trainee solicitors required for 1993: 14
Minimum academic requirements: Second class honours degree. Applications are welcomed from both law and non-law graduates.
Starting salary: £16,000 (September 1990).
Number of qualified solicitors required for 1991: 12-15
Starting salary: Negotiable.
Annual leave entitlement: Four weeks.
Professional development policies and programmes: The firm runs a training programme for all professional staff which includes in-house seminars, and lectures by visiting academics. Trainee solicitors share a room with a partner and work in at least four areas before specializing. They may be seconded abroad.
For brochure and application form contact: William Bale, Partnership Secretary.

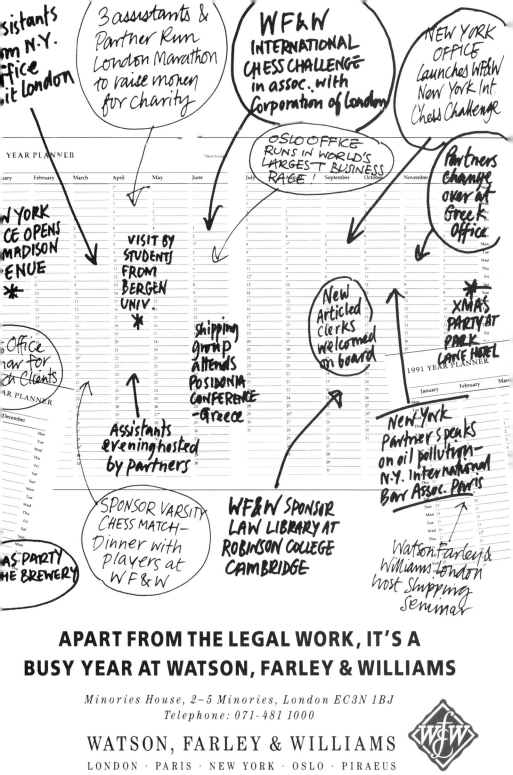

APART FROM THE LEGAL WORK, IT'S A
BUSY YEAR AT WATSON, FARLEY & WILLIAMS

Minories House, 2–5 Minories, London EC3N 1BJ
Telephone: 071-481 1000

WATSON, FARLEY & WILLIAMS
LONDON · PARIS · NEW YORK · OSLO · PIRAEUS

Wilde Sapte

Main office: Queensbridge House, 60 Upper Thames Street, London EC4V 3BD. Tel: 071-236 3050; Telex: 887793 WILDES G; Fax: 071-236 9624.
Other offices and links: The firm has a full service office in New York and extensive links with other law firms throughout the world.
Senior partner: Charles Leeming.
Managing partner: Philip Brown.
Number of partners: 50
Number of staff: 470 (of which 108 are assistant solicitors and 51 are trainee solicitors).
Firm history: Founded in 1785, Wilde Sapte is a leading City commercial practice, representing both UK and overseas clients on a worldwide basis. The firm has expanded rapidly in recent years, doubling in size since 1983. We have developed close working relationships with other international law firms and professions in every major financial centre throughout the world in order to meet clients' needs wherever they arise. In addition, Wilde Sapte has extensive professional contacts in the Middle and Far East. We offer exchange schemes with leading firms in Europe and Japan, and secondments with the European Commission.
Firm structure: The firm comprises five departments – company and commercial, litigation, property, corporate tax, and private client and institutional services. The largest departments are further subdivided into specialist groups, dealing with specific areas of commercial work. In addition, we have Spanish and Japanese speaking units within the firm to serve the particular needs of clients from, or with interests in, those countries. We believe this structure helps us to serve our clients' needs in the most efficient and reliable manner. However, we remain flexible and often assemble hand picked teams for particular tasks, drawing on the firm's resources as a whole.
Major events in the past year: Wilde Sapte has undergone rapid development recently and is committed to growth to enable it to take advantage of the opportunities offered by 1992 and developments within the profession. The firm has continued to strengthen its intellectual property, construction, tax and corporate finance departments. In addition, the firm's outside profile has been significantly raised through its programme of seminars giving major briefings on important areas of business.
Range of client services: The *company and commercial department* offers a full range of services to UK and international public and private companies and to their financial advisers, including the formation of companies, joint ventures, corporate reconstructions, banking, project and asset finance, securities and regulatory matters, flotations and mergers and acquisitions.

Self - Discovery

WILDE SAPTE
UK AND INTERNATIONAL LAWYERS

Queensbridge House, 60 Upper Thames Street, London EC4V 3BD
and in New York.

The *litigation department* consists of over seventy solicitors and other professional staff who handle all aspects of commercial litigation, often international in scope. The department deals with disputes in a number of specialist areas such as construction, banking and finance, insolvency, shipping, aviation, trade, employment and insurance.

The *commercial property department* handles a broad range of work for major companies and institutional clients including the acquisition and disposal of properties, secured lending, planning, institutional investment and joint ventures. The transactions often have significant tax or accounting implications.

Our *corporate tax department*, one of the fastest growing in the firm, works closely with clients' internal tax departments and provides an integrated support service to our other departments.

Finally, the *private client and institutional department* deals with pension schemes and advice, tax planning, UK and international trusts, and inheritance planning. In addition, the department also deals with the needs of major charities.

Number of trainee solicitors required for 1993: Approximately 45.

Minimum academic requirements: A good degree, although not necessarily in law.

Starting salary: £16,250 (September 1990).

Number of qualified solicitors required for 1991: We are always interested in applications from well-qualified solicitors.

Starting salary: £25,000 – newly qualified solicitors (September 1990).

Annual leave entitlement: 20 working days plus extra as service lengthens.

Professional development policies and programmes: It is our policy to invest in broad and well-structured training for all new recruits at whatever level in order to guarantee the firm's future success. Our director of education oversees this. Trainees receive a full induction course including documents and skills training, and 'The City' course which shows how the major institutions work and explains the terminology. There is also a programme of continuing education for everyone through regular seminars and lectures.

For brochure and application form contact: James Curtis for trainees, or Philip Brown for assistant solicitors. Tel: 071-236 3050.